Cities of Stardust, Cities of Blood

Kuğu Tekin

Cities of Stardust, Cities of Blood

London, Venice and İstanbul in Literary Imagination

PETER LANG

Berlin · Bruxelles · Chennai · Lausanne · New York · Oxford

Bibliographic information published by the Deutsche Nationalbibliothek
The German National Library lists this publication in the German
National Bibliography; detailed bibliographic data is available
on the Internet at http://dnb.d-nb.de.

Library of Congress Cataloging-in-Publication Data

Names: Tekin, Kuğu author
Title: Cities of stardust, cities of blood : London, Venice and İstanbul in
   literary imagination / Kuğu Tekin.
Description: Berlin; New York : Peter Lang, 2026. | Includes
   bibliographical references.
Identifiers: LCCN 2025042944 (print) | LCCN 2025042945 (ebook) |
   ISBN 9783631933428 hardback | ISBN 9783631933435 pdf |
   ISBN 9783631933442 epub
Subjects: LCSH: Cities and towns in literature | City and town life in
   literature | Literature and society | London (England)--In literature |
   Venice (Italy)--In literature | Istanbul (Turkey)--In literature |
   LCGFT: Literary criticism
Classification: LCC PN56.C55 T45 2026 (print) | LCC PN56.C55 (ebook) |
   DDC 809/.93321732--dc23/eng/20250929
LC record available at https://lccn.loc.gov/2025042944
LC ebook record available at https://lccn.loc.gov/2025042945

ISBN 978-3-631-93342-8 (Print)
ISBN 978-3-631-93343-5 (ePDF)
ISBN 978-3-631-93344-2 (ePUB)
DOI 10.3726/b23385

www.peterlang.com

Contact for General Product Safety Regulation (GPSR): gpsr@peterlang.com

To my mother, Sabiha and my father, Uğurtan

Contents

Foreword

The ancient and rich histories of London, Venice and İstanbul have been inducing countless authors to produce works related to these cities. During my exploration of the literary production around these three cities, I came to realise that only richly lived experiences allow authors to give full expression to their poetic sensitivity. It would not be too far-fetched to claim that the literary mapping of their beloved cities through a daily immersion into the cities' multifarious lives is also a mapping of their own selves. My literal as well as literary journeys to London, Venice and İstanbul allowed me to understand the perpetual interplay between these iconic cities and authors, and why the distinguished authors selected for this book portray these cities as anthropomorphic figures functioning as major characters in their works.

Preface

The city has been a rich source of inspiration for authors throughout centuries. My intention in writing this book is to present readers with a fresh new perspective focusing on the cityscape and its aesthetic and conceptual ramifications in literary productions. Hence, this book engages in the intertwined relations between the city and authors/poets, their characters and works. To this end, I selected three cities—London, Venice, and İstanbul—to be discussed in three separate chapters. Each of these chapters is divided into three subsections wherein each city is explored through the works of three distinguished authors/poets of different nationalities. For instance, London as the urban landscape is presented through the works of the two English poets, William Blake and William Wordsworth, and a French poet, Arthur Rimbaud. I was particularly attentive to providing readers with diverse movements and genres while structuring the chapters. Following the *Introduction*, the first chapter explores London through a lyric by Blake, a sonnet by Wordsworth, and a prose poem by Rimbaud, organized into three subsections. The second chapter also consists of three works and three subsections on Venice – the first one being a postmodern surrealist novel by the Italian author, Italo Calvino, the second one–a narrative poem by the English poet, Lord Byron, and the last work is a travel sketch by the American modernist author, Henry James. The last chapter is devoted to İstanbul as presented in the works of three Turkish authors. While the first and third subsections introduce two İstanbul poems by Yahya Kemal Beyatlı and by Orhan Veli Kanık, the second subsection engages in Ahmet Hamdi Tanpınar's essay recounting life in İstanbul before and around the early twentieth century. All the chapters and the subsections have an introduction, a conclusion and a discussion comparing the authors' shared views of the city at issue. The conclusion offers a final comparison of the selected authors' diverse impressions and treatments of the cityscape. I hope those who would like to do research and write on the cityscape will find the book inspiring for their future studies.

Acknowledgements

I would like to extend my sincerest gratitude to all my colleagues in the Department of English Language and Literature at Atılım University for their kind support in the writing of this book. I would like to especially thank Professor Oya Batum Menteşe, and our department chair, Professor Nüket Belgin Elbir, for their mentorship and encouragement throughout my academic career. Also, I am deeply indebted to Professor Nüket Belgin Elbir, Professor Aslı Özlem Tarakcioglu, and Dr. Duru Güngör for patiently and meticulously reviewing the manuscript, while I also would like to thank Dr. Zeynep Rana Turgut for her invaluable assistance in research and formatting as well as her steadfast friendship. Sıla Yönden Bağrıyanık, a PhD candidate in our department and my student, was immensely helpful with the formatting of the manuscript, while Esra Bahşi, Senior Commissioning Editor of Peter Lang GmbH, and Sanandita Chanda and Marta Podvolotskaya, my editors, offered their generous support and guidance whenever needed. This work would not have been possible without the boundless affection of my parents, Sabiha and Uğurtan, and my beloved sisters, Ahu and Duru. Finally, I will always remain grateful to my dear spouse, Ahmet, our son Yağız, and our daughter in-law, Yaprak, for their unfaltering affection and care.

Introduction

My journey of exploring the interplay between urban landscapes and authors began with a simple question: What is a city? When and where was it first founded? In a broad sense, a city is defined as

> a bounded space that is densely settled and has a relatively large, culturally hetero-geneous population. The history of cities dates back to the Neolithic period. The oldest known city is Çatal Höyük (7500–5700 BC) in present-day Turkey, while Erbil (founded 6000 BC) in Iraq is the oldest continuously settled city. (Gottdiener, Budd and Lehtovuori 3–4)

Among the many definitions explaining what a city is, I found that of Deyan Sudjic as the most suited for the structure I planned for this book:

> A city is made by its people, within the bounds of the possibilities that it can offer them; it has a distinctive identity that makes it much more than an agglomeration of buildings. Climate, topography and architecture are part of what creates that distinctiveness, as are its origins. ... [I]t is a wealth creating machine that can, at the minimum, make the poor not quite as poor as they were. A real city offers its citizens the freedom to be what they want to be. (1)

However, I noticed that this definition by Sudjic, despite its strengths, over-looks one essential constituent in the making of a real city: art and literature.

While the writer refers to climate, topography, architecture, economy, history, and freedoms and civil rights of citizens as the determining factors of a city's cultural identity, he does not touch upon the role of literature and arts. Evidently, a city's cultural identity, which is shaped mainly by works produced by authors/poets and artists, projects that of its dwellers. A city's cultural formation as a centre of literature and arts is dependent on its capacity to provide authors and artists a libertarian, tolerant environment of production. It appears that, as long as a city provides its dwellers (especially to the underprivileged and disenfranchised groups) with a free, democratic socio-cultural environment, and the required conditions for production in all fields, including literature and fine arts, as well as commodities, such a city will not only maintain its economic power but also enrich its cultural identity. Sudjic gives Amsterdam as a specific example to such cities: '[T]hose cities that exhibited tolerance have flourished ahead of those that have not. Amsterdam became the centre of the world's most powerful trading state in the seventeenth century in part because it encouraged the persecuted – Huguenots, Jews, Puritans and others – to live there' (4). On the other hand, it ought not to be forgotten that, by emulating Amsterdam's urban planning and architecture, rather than its tolerant treatment of communities persecuted elsewhere, Peter the Great built St Petersburg supposedly 'as Russia's window to the world' (Sudjic 5), but without any of the freedoms expected by the modern sensibility. Likewise, such classical cities as Athens, Rome, or the Renaissance Florence lack freedoms and democracy in the modern sense; in fact, according to Sudjic, the architectural design of Moscow, Beijing and Tokyo still reflect the autocracies that built them:

> The Kremlin, the Forbidden City and the Imperial Palace are the monuments of an urban system that was built around a single all-powerful individual. Each of them had a palace at the centre, surrounded by an inner city of retainers and kin, and an outer zone for merchants and labourers excluded from the court. (5)

Obviously, in the past, works of art and literature were produced and disseminated in and around the courts, either by the courtiers themselves, or by those artists and writers who were given the opportunity to work under the patronage of the politically powerful and wealthy nobility. A most notable example of this historical fact would be the burgeoning of the Renaissance-era Florence under the influence of the Medici family.

It is clear that the political power as well as the economic size of a city are among the major factors both determining and refining its cultural identity; since the middle ages, it has been political power accompanied by economic buoyancy that made a city a centre of literature and arts; such are the cities of London, Venice and İstanbul. For instance, London's long-retained status as one of the world's leading financial centres is directly related to the city's political power:

> The political power of cities is related to their position as sites of economic activity. Despite the apparent remorseless march of globalisation and digitisation, certain activities of large transnational firms still crowd into some of the world's major cities. The benefits of co-location are expressed as agglomeration economies[1] in the form of specialist labour markets, transport accessibility and access to shared lifestyle aspirations. The city of London retains its position as one of the world's leading financial centres as a result of these agglomeration benefits. (Gottdiener, Budd and Lehtovuori 3)

Since the concept of the cityscape and its representation in literature have always fascinated me, I wrote a number of essays, articles, and book chapters on the subject. Among these, in an article on Venice, I examined the representations of Venice, the so-called 'mercurial city', with reference to the works of Thomas Mann, Jeanette Winterson and Kazuo Ishiguro. For instance, 'Jan' is the protagonist in Ishiguro's short story titled 'Crooner'. He is a young Polish guitarist who is trying to earn a living as a street musician in Venice. He accompanies various bands with his guitar as needed to entertain the tourists in Piazza San Marco. Regarding Jan's temporary residence in Venice, the adjective 'mercurial' denotes a potential for an unpredictable change in mood and mind or fortune; it is also a reference to the amphibious, fluid nature of Venice, a city well-known to challenge all the fixed rules and

---

[1] Agglomeration economies exist when production is cheaper because of this clustering of economic activity. As a result of this clustering, it becomes possible to establish other businesses that may take advantage of these economies without joining any large organisation. This process may help to urbanise areas as well. Urbanisation and the trade of goods and services often go parallel. Cities benefit from agglomeration economies' external benefits that arise when economic activity takes place in a concentrated space. The spatial nature of London's economy is the product of more than two centuries of trade and agglomeration at work (Kumar 9).

norms that limit individuals' material and psychological advancement. The character-moulding power of the amphibious, fluid Venice could also be traced in Jeanette Winterson's protagonist, Villanelle, in *The Passion*. Venice, the city she was born in, granted Villanelle the magical ability to walk on the Adriatic Sea with her webbed feet. At the end, Villanelle is portrayed as a free Venetian woman, a single mother who rebels against all sorts of prejudices limiting women in the late eighteenth century. However, the ending of Ishiguro's story presents Jan as an outsider whose fate in Venice seems frozen, parallel to the concerted efforts of Venetians and tourists to freeze the city in an overly romanticised yet increasingly vacant illusion – the living, mercurially fluid city being gradually replaced by an unmoving, unchanging, lifeless museum piece built to satisfy commercially triggered nostalgia. As for Thomas Mann's novella, *Death in Venice*, the city is drawn like a death trap with its labyrinthine, dark and narrow cholera-ridden streets, gateways and alleys. Mann's ironic description of 'La Serenissima', in a sense, confirms the city's fame as a magical site casting its spell on its visitors; yet, the city's magic affects the protagonist, Gustave Von Aschenbach, a distinguished, widely acclaimed German writer, in the worst possible way. Mann's Venice, in a sense, acts like an antagonist leading Aschenbach firstly to his physical and psychological breakdown, and ultimately to his tragic death.[2]

In the second chapter of this present book, I continue with this exploration of Venice the magical city, this time with reference to Italo Calvino's *Invisible Cities*, Lord Byron's 'Canto IV Venice', and the Venice section of Henry James's *Italian Hours*. The first chapter is dedicated to London, and the last, to İstanbul, as two other great cities that have exerted as much influence on literary minds as Venice. For instance, regarding London, Peter Ackroyd's novel, *Dan Leno and the Limehouse Golem*, which is set in Victorian London in the 1880s, presents the cityscape as a site perpetually inspiring, encouraging, and triggering the main character's impulse to kill.[3] The first chapter

---

² Tekin, Kuğu. 'Marginalised Flaneurs in Venice in the Works of Mann, Winterson and Ishiguro'. *Synergy I: Marginalisation, Discrimination, Isolation and Existence in Literature*. Peter Lang pp. 95–115, 2021.

³ Tekin, Kuğu. 'Mapping London in Peter Ackroyd's *Dan Leno and the Limehouse Golem*: Promenades into a Murderer's Mind'. Ankara University: Journal of the Faculty of Languages and History-Geography. 58 (2), 2018, pp. 1522–1534. <https://doi.org/10.33171/dtcfjournal.2018.58.2.17-ISSN:2459-0150>.

of the present book offers readers three other literary portraits of London, Londoners, and ways of living in the eighteenth-century through William Blake's 'London', William Wordsworth's 'Composed upon Westminster Bridge', and Arthur Rimbaud's 'The Bridges', respectively.

The last city to be explored in the third chapter is İstanbul; the focus is on two poems by Yahya Kemal Beyatlı and Orhan Veli Kanık, titled 'From another Hill' and 'I am listening to İstanbul', as well as a long essay, 'İstanbul', from Ahmet Hamdi Tanpınar's collection of essays, *Five Cities*. In a nutshell, my intention in writing this book is to take the audience to a literary journey woven out of the dreams and bitter truths revolving around these three urban landscapes as envisioned by my selected authors.

London

> 'His Return to London'
> From the dull confines of the drooping West,
> To see the day spring from the pregnant East,
> Ravished in spirit, I come, nay more, I fly
> To thee, blest place of my nativity!
> London my home is, though by hard fate sent
> Into a long and irksome banishment;
> Yet since called back, henceforward let me be,
> O native country, repossessed by thee![4]
> —HERRICK (1366)

This chapter explores the intimate relationship between the city of London and three distinguished poets who produced their works in the late eighteenth and nineteenth centuries. The poets of this section, namely William Blake, William Wordsworth and Arthur Rimbaud, offer their specific views of London from such a refined literary and philosophical perspective that their works have become an indispensable source for scholars investigating urban studies. Three works by these poets will be examined chronologically, focusing on their structural and thematic traits. Accordingly, the first London poem to be analysed is William Blake's 'London'.

---

[4]   Robert Herrick's seventeenth-century poem, 'His Return to London' reflects the poet's profound sense of delight springing from his return to London, to the blessed city of his birth (Abrams, *Norton* 1366).

1.1 William Blake's 'London'

William Blake (1757–1827) published his poem 'London' in 1794. The poem is taken from Blake's collection titled *Songs of Experience* (1794), and it is one of the few poems which does not have an equivalent in the poet's previously published collection titled *Songs of Innocence* (1789). As the sequential titles of the two collections suggest, Blake left behind his highly optimistic view of nature, of man, of joy and of civil rights in *Songs of Experience*. In the poem titled 'London', Blake reflects his disappointment, his vanished hopes of establishing a free, peaceful, prosperous future and an egalitarian and just rule the poet believed Londoners deserved. According to literary historians, Blake's disappointment is closely linked to the brutal aftereffects of the 1789 French Revolution in that the poet personally witnessed the reverberations of the failure of the Revolution's motto, 'liberty, equality, fraternity', in the capital of his own country. The ideology behind Blake's poetic and artistic oeuvre stems from an acute political awareness of the social and economic problems of his time. Janet Sayers and Nanette Monin's article titled 'Blake's 'London': Diabolical reading and poetic place in organisational theorising', reflects upon the consequences of both the French Revolution and the Industrial Revolution on the Blakean aesthetics. The two critics' research on the biography and the impact of the groundbreaking national and international events on the artist's life and work reads as follows:

> [William Blake] was a poet, painter and print-maker and was also a Londoner who lived through the massive social and economic upheavals of the Industrial Revolution as experienced in the UK and the international political tensions caused by the French Revolution. He often subsisted in poverty, and was a first-hand witness to the social degradation caused by rapid industrialisation in London. His work had political and humanitarian purposes as he was concerned to alleviate suffering in his community of souls. (2)

Songs of Innocence, which was a product of Blake's early artistic career, consists of poems that foreshadow the typical Romantic attitude of worshipping the joy found only in the natural world, aspiring to attain innocence and a closer relationship with God. Nevertheless, contrary to the joyous mood of the poems in Songs of Innocence which 'were written from the perspective of children or written about them' (Sayers & Monin 3), in *Songs of Experience,* Blake drew a very dark and gloomy picture of humanity, of the urban landscape resulting from the malpractices of politicians, poverty, and the bitter class-based social and religious dissensions of the times. In 'Eighteenth-Century London: Urban Paradise or Fallen City?', Arthur J. Weitzman mentions several eighteenth-century thinkers'/authors' opposing views comparing urban life to country life; in the article, London is the urban centre, the metropolis, and its antithesis is the British countryside. For instance, while to William Blake, who was a resident of London, his fellow citizens 'were suffering from a spiritual malaise', a foreign observer from Germany, as Weitzman quotes, wrote with great admiration that the liberty in the eighteenth-century London could not be found elsewhere in the world:

> There is no place in the world where a man may live according to his own mind, or even his whim, than in London. For this reason, I believe that in no place are to be found a greater variety of original characters … The friend of art and science, the friend of religious liberty, the philosopher, the man who wishes to be secure against political and ecclesiastical tyrants, the man of business, the man of pleasure, can nowhere be better off than in this metropolis…. A man of learning, who can live without great cares, may gratify here his favourite inclinations, for libraries, for new publications, for learned acquaintance.[5] (Wendeborn quoted in Weitzman 472)

It is seen that the German writer particularly praised, indeed envied, the intellectual freedom artists, thinkers and scientists enjoyed in London; this sense of freedom in the metropolis, the foreign-observer thought, offered all the opportunities required for the creative process of philosophical, artistic and scientific endeavours. As a result, Wendeborn claimed, London hosted miscellaneous original authors, artists and intellectuals, and thus, became the world's central metropolis even as early as the eighteenth-century. It might be possible to say that the later Romantics' discontent with the city life owes much to Blake, who juxtaposed the mythic cities of Jerusalem[6] with

---

[5]   Wendeborn, Friedrich A. A View of England Towards the Close of the Eighteenth Century. Vol. 1, London, 1791, pp. 257–69.

[6]   The City of Jerusalem is sacred to many religious traditions. Abrahamic religions of Judaism, Christianity and Islam consider it a holy city.

Babylon[7] in his work. Weitzman relates the sharp distance between urban life and rural life initially to materialism that gained an immense impetus with the advancement of industrialism, and to the erosion of spiritual values: 'In the eighteenth century there was a progressive disenchantment with the metropolis as it appeared to lose its innocence and divine approbation because of its secularisation and commitment to purely social and economic values' (472). Likewise, in his poem 'London', Blake frankly conveys his critique of and discontent with the social, economic and political oppression of the authorities; the corruption of the institutions like the Anglican church, which deliberately remained indifferent to the sufferings of those in need; the relentless practices of child labour; and the social injustice to which Londoners, especially commoners, were exposed. Michael Ferber starts his article by describing the site where one can read the inscription of Blake's 'London':

> If you cross the Thames on Westminster Bridge from Parliament to the south bank, go down the stairs on the left side, and walk a hundred yards or so you will come upon the text of Blake's great short poem 'London' chiselled into the stone pavement. It is a good place to read the poem, in sight of the chartered Thames it speaks of and not far from Blake's home in Lambeth where he wrote it. (Ferber 310)

William Blake's lyric, consisting of four quatrains with alternate lines rhyming, is as follows:

'London'
I wander thro' each charter'd street,
Near where the charter'd Thames does flow.
And mark in every face I meet
Marks of weakness, marks of woe

In every cry of every Man,
In every Infants cry of fear,
In every voice: in every ban,
The mind-forg'd manacles I hear

How the Chimney-sweepers cry
Every blackning Church appals,

---

[7] Originating from the exile of Israelites from Jerusalem, Babylon has come to incorporate notions of evil, oppression and corruption.

And the hapless Soldiers sigh
Runs in blood down Palace walls

But most thro' midnight streets I hear
How the youthful Harlot's curse
Blasts the new-born Infants tear
And blights with plagues the Marriage hearse. (39)

As is seen, the setting in the opening is the urban landscape depicted at night. The speaker is wandering around the darkened streets of London, observing marks of pain and despair on the faces of each Londoner he encounters. The word 'chartered' appearing in the first two lines of the poem is a reference to the politically oppressed Londoners in that freedom of thought and speech was banned and controlled by means of 'charters'.[8] The chartered waters of the Thames denote the tyranny prevailing in the city. Through the use of the repetitive words in the second quatrain, Blake powerfully voices the cry of the suffering Londoners. 'Mind-forged manacles' in the last line is a reference to the legal sanctions restricting human soul and imagination. In the following quatrain criticism is directed at the child labour, the church and English monarchy. The poet draws attention to the unheard voices of children who become the cheap working force to be mercilessly exploited in the hands of the newly emerging middle-class entrepreneurs. Sayers and Monin Sayers state,

> 'Mind-forged manacles' imprisoning the spirits and bodies of Londoners suggest the fires of huge nineteenth century factories and their filthy chimneys; the industrial power of a city that has been blackened … by the corrupt morality of the owners and managers whose wealth is built on the backs of abused workers. (4)

In the third quatrain, two institutions, namely the church and the government ('palace') have become the centre of Blake's severe criticism in that the church is frightening the believers instead of relieving them. The church is supposed to do charity and to alleviate the spiritual pain of the suffering Londoners. Nevertheless, the church in London is appalling and what makes the church 'appalling' is its indifferent stance against the misery of Londoners.

---

[8]   Charters were given to people who were either richer or more powerful than others and that licence allowed them to control the streets of London.

This quatrain also refers to the unlucky soldiers whose blood reddened the walls of the Palace. To Blake, the evil doings of the wicked rulers, the strategic blunders they made, led to the destruction of a whole generation of young soldiers. It is also noteworthy in this quatrain that the critique of the institutions of power are made through the use of synecdoche[9] in that the clergy and the ruling authorities are criticised by the places in which they reside. Sayer and Monin's comment on the corruption of the church and the power-stricken politicians reads as follows:

> In the midst of this spiritually and physically black city run streaks of red. The red blood of the soldier, running 'down palace walls' symbolises the physical destruction of London's citizens in the wealth and power pursuit of government and parallels the black destruction wrought by the Church. (5)

Blake's use of colour symbolism not only poeticises the miserable condition of his fellow Londoners but also specifies the site and source of corruption in the city. The last quatrain is set at midnight and the only voice the speaker hears in the midst of darkness is the young 'harlot's curse', which is a direct reference to young women who are forced to prostitution for they have no other means to survive. As Blake prophecies, the helpless young woman's curse would be an epidemic which would undoubtedly sicken the posterity. As for the last two lines, here Blake juxtaposes the institution of marriage with death. 'Marriage hearse' in the last line paradoxically combines the two concepts for a hearse, as is well-known, is a vehicle used to carry the coffin at a funeral. The poet's combination of the two concepts indicates that marriage, which is traditionally associated with procreation and continuity, is unfruitful and sterile in London where death is stalking in the streets to hunt its unlucky, destitute inhabitants. In Weitzman's words, 'the city was a dead ideal-a Babylon to Blake', (480) for the poet's bleak vision presents an eighteenth-century London whose disadvantaged inhabitants are living a hellish life under the constant threat of poverty, violence and death.

---

[9] Synecdoche is a literary device in which a part of something is substituted for the whole.

1.2 William Wordsworth's London

This section of the book holds a discussion on the idealised beauty of London as described by the nineteenth-century Romantic poet William Wordsworth (1770–1850) in his Petrarchan sonnet titled 'Composed upon Westminster Bridge, September 3, 1802'. While the first section of the book presents William Blake's lyric demonstrating a dark, pessimistic, even horrifying vision of London, this second section deals with William Wordsworth's sonnet which presents a rather positive London image. The comparison of the two poets' distinctive approaches to the cityscape will go in parallel with the analysis of the sonnet.

'Composed upon Westminster Bridge, September 3, 1802'
Earth has not anything to show more fair:
Dull would he be of soul who could pass by
A sight so touching in its majesty:
This City now doth, like a garment, wear
The beauty of the morning; silent, bare,
Ships, towers, domes, theatres, and temples lie
Open unto the fields, and to the sky;
All bright and glittering in the smokeless air.
Never did sun more beautifully steep
In his first splendour, valley, rock, or hill;
Ne'er saw I, never felt, a calm so deep!
The river glideth at his own sweet will:
Dear God! the very houses seem asleep;
And all that mighty heart is lying still! (198)

The opening of the sonnet presents the speaker standing on the Westminster bridge early in the morning, stunned by the serene beauty of the city scenery extending before his eyes. This majestic sight of the urban landscape raises profound emotions in the speaker. The personified city is asleep, and the silence of the early morning enhances its beauty. Here, the persona visualises the city as a sleeping beauty whose attire is made of 'the beauty of the morning'. In 'William Blake and William Wordsworth's Reactions to the Industrial Revolution, Özge Güvenç states that when the metropolis – 'the sleeping beauty' – wakes up, the speaker's enchanted condition would turn into disappointment: '... in a few hours the city will wake up and this beauty will culminate in industrial work including noise and pollution' (120). Güvenç's comment on the Romantics' dislike of leading a mechanised, soulless life in a chaotic city where everything is calculated and designed for profit maximisation of capital owners parallels Weitzman's argument based on the Romantic nature/culture dilemma:

> [The Romantics] would have liked to live in an idealised classical city, an Athens or Augustan Rome of their imagination-a city of culture in the truest sense. Yet the noise and perpetual whirl of commercial and criminal London kept closing on them. They couldn't really reconcile the two images, although one has a sense of their having tried desperately to do so. It remained for the Romantics utterly to reject the city as a meaningless and trivial experience. In Wordsworth's vision, London was topsy-turvy, oppressive, and irredeemable. (Güvenç 479)

However, contrary to Weitzman's views, the very lines of the sonnet prove that Wordsworth achieved a perfect nature/culture balance, a harmonious connection between natural life and modern man's city experience in 'Composed upon Westminster Bridge September 3, 1802'. Matthew Sangster's article titled 'Coherence and Inclusion in the Life Writing of Romantic-period London' dwells on the theme of the representations of individual lives in the burgeoning city of London in the works of a diverse range of Romantic-period authors and artists through implicitly and explicitly evoking the lives lived within it' (142). According to Sangster,

> Late eighteenth- and early nineteenth-century literary works commonly seem either to recoil from London – as is the case with many novels that dip into the city but begin and end in more comprehensible communities at a distance from it – or to censure the metropolis, imagining it as an oppressor or a trap, as William Blake does in 'London' … (143)

Obviously, the Romantic authors needed to distance themselves from the crowded city in order to overcome their artistic anxieties concerning the ways to achieve poetic perfection in the expression of the self and a truer expression of a life experience lived within the city. While a strong sense of fear dominates the streets and lives of Londoners in Blake's 'London', in 'The Prelude', Wordsworth defines the feeling that both London and its dwellers evoke in him as 'mystery' (Sangster 143). It seems that since the densely populated London of the 1800s and the miscellany of characters inhabiting the metropolis caused a kind of lethargic effect on Wordsworth's imaginative skills, the poet preferred to cast a distant gaze upon London and the related city image he wished to compose. In Sangster's words:

London overwhelms [Wordsworth] because it contains too many lives lived in parallel. It is only through retreating and setting the city in its natural contexts, as he does in the 1802 sonnet 'Composed Upon Westminster Bridge', that he can definitively characterise it, […] London is an awkward location for Wordsworth's modes of life writing because its profusion of potential signifiers overwhelms the clusters of meaning through which he tries to define his own self-worth. While he is not wholly negative about the city, he ultimately delineates his own existence in large part through the rejection of metropolitan experiences. (144)

Hence, it is inferred that Wordsworth's positive description of the silent solitude and the sense of 'calmness' inspired by the early hours of a London morning in 'Composed Upon Westminster Bridge' definitely stands in contrast with Blake's bleak city image which could be traced in the fear stricken faces of every Londoner the speaker encounters in the poem 'London'. In fact, Blake's bleak London vision rather predicts that of William Cobbett (1763–1835), the English journalist, author and politician, who called London in the wake of Industrial era 'the Great Wen, a tumour on the face of rural England', as was the fashion among 'the observers of modern cities using metaphors of sickness and disease in their city descriptions in the 1830s' (Sudjic 5). Along with the Industrial era, the rural rush into the urban metropolis for a better future ended the naive intact pastoral life in the British countryside. As Blake states in his 'Jerusalem'[10]: England's green and pleasant land had been overwhelmed by 'dark satanic mills'[11] that diminished the lives of the rural communities that flocked into the big cities to find work' (Sudjic 175). According to Sudjic, many in Britain were overwhelmed by the idea of the modern city that emerged along with the Industrial Revolution. For instance:

…author William Morris (1834–1896) and those who thought like him, identified big cities with all that had gone wrong with the world. […] In his novel News

---

[10] Please, see appendix A for the full text of the poem.

[11] Blake employs 'dark satanic mills' as a metaphor to illustrate the destructive impact of the early Industrial Revolution on nature and human relationships in his 1808 poem titled 'Jerusalem'.

from Nowhere, Morris portrayed a London deserted after the fall of capitalism. Parliament Square is transformed into a dung heap, with worthless banknotes fluttering in the wind. The city's inhabitants have dispersed into the countryside to live the life of nineteenth-century hippies. (Sudjic 175)

Despite such facilities as street lighting and a suburban railway system brought about by modernity, cholera became a deadly threat in London almost throughout the nineteenth-century. The city was suffering from a serious cholera epidemic caused by contaminated water:

> The Thames was an open sewer responsible for the so-called 'Great Stink'; so noxious in its effects that parliamentarians in the hot summer of 1858 kept the windows of the newly completed Houses of Parliament tightly shut to keep out the smell. The stench was crippling, but the real danger, the accompanying cholera outbreaks, was only dealt with by Bazalgette's[12] new sewers and pumping stations, built between 1865 and 1875. Even then [...] the East End[13] of London is the hell of poverty. Like one enormous giant kraken, the poverty of London lies there in lurking silence and encircles with its mighty tentacles the life and wealth of the City. (Sudjic 175)

As one might expect, the environmental catastrophes London underwent throughout the late eighteenth and nineteenth-centuries naturally triggered 'the nostalgia for a green and pleasant land is felt strongly through John Constable's (1776–1837) painting, *The Hay Wain*, as well as through William Cobett's book, *Rural Rides* that has until recently created an anti-urban culture and promoted the ideal of suburbia' (Gottdiener, Budd, and Lehtovuori 5).

Coming back to the issue, the poetic persona in Wordsworth's sonnet opines that this panoramic view of the city whose name is not mentioned in the poem is blending with nature and this very scenery manifests itself as the harmony between nature, man and the city. Wordsworth's allusions to the industrial London as the first and most crowded metropolis could be

---

12 Sir Joseph William Bazalgette (1819–1891) was a British civil engineer who designed the main drainage system for London. <https://www.britannica.com>

13 In June 1866, a localised epidemic in the East End of London claimed 5596 lives, just as the city was completing construction of its major sewage and water treatment systems: the East End section was not quite complete. <https://www.nationalarchives.gov.uk>

followed in the octave in line six referring to 'ships, towers, domes, theatres and temples', yet it is observed in the following seventh and eighth lines that all these man-made constructions, which are considered to be the vast scope of man's technological advancement, open into nature, into 'fields glittering under the smokeless air' of the 'bright sky'. The typical Romantic idea contends that along with the Industrial Revolution man lost his contact with nature. Nevertheless, the lines of the sestet portraying the speaker in an ecstatic state of tranquillity evidenced that Wordsworth was not entirely hostile to the urban landscape like his fellow Romantic poets. The 'mighty heart' in the last line is a metaphor Wordsworth used for London. The exclamation marks employed in the last two lines indicate the sublimity of both the speaker's and the poet's feelings evoked by the magnificent city spectacle. Hence, it might be claimed that this sonnet is a manifestation of Wordsworth's reconciliation with the industrialised urban landscape for his confession voiced by the poetic persona declares that that specific London morning has made him feel a deeper sense of serenity than he has ever experienced elsewhere.

Regarding the comparison of the two London poems by William Blake and William Wordsworth, Bernard O'Keeffe in 'London' and 'Composed upon Westminster Bridge' investigates the parallels and differences between the two poets' treatment of the city. It is seen that London is the common subject of both poets; however, O'Keeffe claims, Wordsworth's optimistic, glorifying tone and attitude towards the city appear to be the exact opposite of Blake's whose dark London image is resonating with the cries of the oppressed, abused, deprived sufferers. Concerning the contradictory feelings the two poems evoke in the audience, O'Keeffe claims:

> Whereas Blake's poem seems to be a cry of despair at the suffering he sees and hears around him, Wordsworth's appears to be a eulogy, seeing in the early-morning London scene a beauty that surpasses the majesty and awe of the natural landscapes with which he is normally associated. While Blake's poem is concerned with the painful effects that institutions of power have on the individual, Wordsworth's is focused on the surprising beauty of the early-morning scene and the calm it induces in him. (21)

Apart from differences, there are conceptual affinities between the two distinguished poets of the Romantic era. On the ideologies and typical thematic characteristics adopted and shared by all the Romantic poets, including Blake and Wordsworth, O'Keeffe writes:

> the effect of the world on the poet's own emotional state and feelings, a concern with the freedom of the individual and a veneration of nature, natural states and the innocence associated with them. (22)

In 'Sign, Sensation and the Body in Wordsworth's Residence in London', C. R. Stokes attributes to eighteenth century London a pioneering role concerning the representation of modern man's urban experience in literature. According to Stokes, the spatialities and temporalities provided by London as a metropolis of the time enabled Wordsworth to compose an 'epic representation' of the individual's experiences of the urban landscape:

> …the type of epic metropolis represented by Wordsworth's London was unique at the time, proleptic of a whole century of mass urbanisation. Where the 1801 census registered over a million Londoners, it would take Paris until the 1840s to reach that mark, and Berlin and Vienna until the 1870s and 1880s respectively. (207)

In brief, the Romantics' early modes of writings about man's experience of the cityscape paved the way to the later development of 'the most fully-fledged critical vocabularies [and theories]' based on urban studies (Stokes 207). One last remark on William Wordsworth's 'Composed upon Westminster Bridge' might be that the poet succeeded in capturing a moment and envision a modern man who is still tightly holding his ties with nature, even in the midst of the then largest industrial metropolis.

1.3 Arthur Rimbaud's London

This section of the first chapter discusses this time a French poet's views on London in the nineteenth-century. While the first two sections of this chapter dwell on the two British poets' poems, William Blake's lyric, and William Wordsworth's sonnet, this section will focus on the impressions London left on the French poet, Arthur Rimbaud's (1854–1891) prose poem titled 'The Bridges'. Prior to the discussion of the relationship between the City-London-and the way the foreign poet perceived the city, it might be helpful to give brief information on Rimbaud, his art, the 'Decadence movement' and the definition of the term 'prose poem'.

Decadents were a group of late nineteenth and early twentieth-century writers who produced their works principally in France but also in England and America. The origins of the movement dated back to the literature of Hellenistic Greece and to Roman literature. These literatures were said to embody 'the high refinements and subtle beauties of a culture and art which have passed their vigorous prime, but manifest a special, sweet savour or incipient decay' (Abrams, *Glossary* 42–43). The precepts of the Decadent movement, whose leading representative in France is Charles Baudelaire, read as follows:

> Central to the movement was that art is totally opposed to nature, in the sense both of biological nature and of the standard, or natural, norms of morality and sexual behaviour. [...] the Decadent writer cultivates high artifice in his style and, often, the bizarre in his subject matter, recoils from the fecundity and exuberance of the organic and instinctual life of nature, prefers elaborate dress over the living form and cosmetics over the natural hue, and sometimes [...] violate what is commonly held to be natural in human experience by resorting to drugs, deviancy, or sexual experimentation [...] to achieve [in Rimbaud's words] 'the systematic derangement of all the senses'. (Abrams, Glossary 43)

The Decadent authors commonly held the idea that art was superior and that the finest beauty could be found in dying or decaying things. Another common characteristic of the Decadent artists was that they attacked the social and moral standards of their time with their lifestyles as well as with their artistic and literary productions. The leading exponents of the movement in France were Verlaine, Rimbaud, Baudelaire and Huysmans; in England, the Decadents were Oscar Wilde, Ernest Dowson, Aubrey Beardsley and Frank Harris.

Arthur Rimbaud had a very short literary career. He started writing when he was 15 and abandoned poetry when he was only 19. Yet, the body of his work exerted enormous influence upon future poets with the publication of his *Illuminations*. The innovative, even revolutionary characteristics of Rimbaud's poetics and his notion of how the poet should be are as follows:

> Rimbaud appealed to the visual component of imagination
>
> (his 'Voyelles' compares vowels with colours and images), described his poetics as a form of self-induced vision, arguing that the poets must make themselves voyants (seers) through a purposeful 'disordering of the senses'. In this way poetry will no longer relate actions in rhyme but will itself occur 'in advance of them', vision thus creating experience. (Preminger 1089)

Rimbaud's idea of the poet as the voyant (the seer) might be explained with reference to his famous 'agrammatical dictum, 'car Je est un autre' (for I is another),[14] by which the self, identified by being 'disordered' with what is not the self, acquires the double (creative and reflective) vision of the voyant' (Preminger 1089). Rimbaud's work combines a cynical realism and an attempt to transform both self and surroundings into a magically perfect whole. In Illuminations his aim was to create a state of natural innocence and harmony. Nevertheless, before moving to the discussion on the poet's 'The Bridges' which is taken from The Illuminations, one explanation of the defining characteristics of the term 'prose poem' appears to be necessary:

> The extreme conventions of 18th-c. French neoclassicism, with its strict rules for the differentiation of poetry from prose, are to be blamed for the controversially hybrid and (aesthetically and even politically) revolutionary genre of the prose poem. With its oxymoronic title and its form based on contradiction, the prose poem is suitable to an extraordinary range of perception and expression, from the ambivalent (in content as in form) to the mimetic and the narrative (or even anecdotal). … Its principal characteristics insure unity even in brevity and poetic quality even without the line breaks of free verse: high patterning, rhythmic and figural repetition, sustained intensity, and compactness. (Prminger 977)

Arthur Rimbaud's prose poem is as follows:

'The Bridges'

Crystalline gray skies. A strange pattern of bridges, these straight, those arched, others descending obliquely at angles to the first, and these configurations repeating themselves in the other circuits of the canal, but all so long and light that the shores, laden with domes, sink and diminish. Some of these bridges are still encumbered with hovels. Others support masts, signals, frail parapets. Minor chords interweave, and flow smoothly; ropes rise from the steep banks. One detects a red jacket, perhaps other costumes and musical instruments. Are these popular tunes, fragments of manorial concerts, remnants of public anthems? The water is gray and blue, ample as an arm of the sea. A white ray, falling from the summit of the sky, reduces to nothingness this theatrical performance. (Mack 1179)

As is said, this is a prose poem written in free verse. The poem conveys an impressionistic memory of London through transfigured scenes taken from

---

[14] *I* is somebody else.

the city's real life. Rimbaud transforms this everyday reality by means of the recreative power of poetry. The speaker who presents himself as 'the seer' is contemplating upon the bridges of London extending along the shores of the river Thames. The poet's approach to London, resembling that of a synesthete, is musical in that the poem achieves an orchestral quality while words suggest and mingle colour and sound impressions. In 'Radical Realism: Rimbaud's Affinities with Impressionism' Aimée Israel-Pelletier states that: 'Rimbaud's frequent allusions to a sort of merging of sounds and colours is used as evidence of his affinities with Impressionist art' (59–60). To Pelletier, the lines 'Minor chords interweave, and flow smoothly; ropes rise from the steep banks. One detects a red jacket, perhaps other costumes and musical instruments' confirm her idea that 'The Bridges' is the Impressionist poem 'par excellence'; it is a fantasmagorical vision inspired by Rimbaud's stay in London' (60).

The reason why Rimbaud implemented an unconventional versification technique, unorthodox logic, and a specific coherence in the *Illuminations* in general, and in 'The Bridges' in particular, is related to the poet's desire to create an idiosyncratic sense of reality. Consequently, Rimbaud followed the path of Impressionist painters to achieve his ultimate purpose:

> Just as the Impressionists thought it would be impossible to paint mobility and the transience of light and its changing effects on the landscape by following the techniques used by the Realists before them, so Rimbaud also could not describe the feeling of contentment [, or discontentment], of excitement or of confusion, the tumult of a city … by using conventional forms and techniques. (Pelletier 67)

Regarding the impact of modern urban life on Rimbaud's Illuminations, Greg Kerr writes:

> As he demonstrates in other poems from Illuminations, commerce, transportation, monumental construction, and other facets of modern urban life both accelerate and consolidate the subject's confrontation with the objects and images of his desire and with the collective aspirations of the metropolis. ('Rhetorics of Transformation' in Rimbaud's Illuminations 28)

Coming back to the interpretation of the poem, it appears that on considering the main function of a bridge which is to conjoin two separate shores, one might first think that the poem is alluding to the far-reaching power of the

British empire which has connected to, and brought near to itself, countless countries in several continents in the nineteenth-century. Those bridges were made of steel, and steel is often used as the symbol of the Industrial Revolution. Therefore, a possible interpretation might be that those very 'long and light' bridges which seem to be floating in the air, reflect a kind of disbelief in man's progress. The audience also notices an implicit allusion to the decline of the British empire upon which the sun is supposed never to set. There is a slight reference to the fading British nationalism as well. The poet puts emphasis on the fleeting nature of all this display of magnificence. The impression London leaves on the poet is transience of magnificence, and, in this respect, one might draw a parallel between Rimbaud's 'The Bridges' and the speech given by Shakespeare's Prospero in The Tempest in Act 4 scene 1:

> You do look, my son, in a moved sort,
> As if you were dismay'd: be cheerful, sir.
> Our revels now are ended. These our actors,
> As I foretold you, were all spirits and
> Are melted into air, into thin air:
> And, like the baseless fabric of this vision,
> The cloud-capp'd towers, the gorgeous palaces,
> The solemn temples, the great globe itself,
> Ye all which it inherits, shall dissolve
> And, like this insubstantial pageant faded,
> Leave not a rack behind. We are such stuff
> As dreams are made on, and our little life
> Is rounded with a sleep … (Shakespeare 19)

Concerning the creation/destruction binary on which Rimbaud grounded the Illuminations and the final sentence of 'The Bridges' David Berry writes:

> …the dialectical pattern of creation followed by destruction that will become a central creative process in the Illuminations. In 'Les Ponts', for example, the scene of bridges which is transformed by a certain shaft of sunlight into a glittering theatrical decor of unexpected perspectives and criss-crossing planes is annihilated when the light changes: 'Un rayon blanc, tomb ant du haut du ciel, aneantir cette comedie'.[15] ('Thematics of Hunger and Thirst in Rimbaud's Poetry' 90)

---

[15] A white ray falling from the summit of the sky, reduces to nothingness this theatrical performance.

Obviously, the London scenery extending before the poet's eyes is beautiful, yet this beauty is a decaying, even dying one. As is observed, Rimbaud's poem conveys the city impressions of an outsider; his attitude towards London appears to be distant and neutral compared to those of Blake and Wordsworth. Rimbaud's 'The Bridges' pictures the nineteenth-century London's social and even political life from a realistic perspective. However, some of Rimbaud readers argued that his language is marked by obscurity. The reason for this misjudgement is likely to be Rimbaud's distinct sense of reality and his unconventional medium to present it in his work including 'The Bridges'. Thus, the body of Rimbaud's work embodying the London image which the poet drew and coloured with the refined aesthetic sense of an impressionist painter has become one of the forerunners of modernist poetry.

Venice

Beneath is spread like a green sea
The waveless plain of Lombardy,
Bounded by the vaporous air,
Islanded by cities fair;
Underneath Day's azure eyes
Ocean's nursling, Venice lies,
A peopled labyrinth of walls,
Amphitrite's destin'd halls,
Which her hoary sire now paves
With his blue and beaming waves.
—SHELLEY (117)

The second chapter investigates three works which are set in Venice, alternatively called either 'the queen of the Adriatic', or 'La Serenissima'. The first subsection analysing the intertwined connection between authors-characters and the cityscape focuses on 'Italo Calvino's (1923–1985) representation of Venice in his book titled *Invisible Cities* (1972); the second subsection dwells on Lord Byron's (1788–1824) travelogue titled *Childe Harold's Pilgrimage*; nevertheless, I give specific attention to Canto IV Venice which recounts the city's great monuments, emblems, relics and the poet's impressions concerning the fading glory of the rich city state. Lastly, the third author, whose impressions of Venice are analysed in the third subsection of this chapter, is Henry James (1843-1916); the focus is on the Venice section of his travel sketch titled *Italian Hours*. The thematic analyses of the three works based on the three authors' distinct views and descriptions of the urban landscape, also include the structural features. My intention is to convey the reader a holistic approach while introducing the city, Venice, which has inspired countless authors, artists, and musicians throughout centuries. Venice has been a site of attraction with its very special topography and geographical location where the sensuality and exoticism of the East and the rationality of the West blend, with its 118 islands, with its grand architectural structures-palaces, statues, cathedrals, piazzas, bridges and canals, maze-like narrow, dark alleys – each of which keeping a secret of ancient times, and with its rich historical and cultural heritage. The city's economic status is also significant due to its being a centre of commerce in that starting from the early middle ages up to Napoleon's invasion of the city (1797) the riches of the East poured into Venice incessantly.

2.1 Italo Calvino's Venice

Italo Calvino's introduction of his notion of the city and his book *Invisible Cities* is as follows:

> A city is a combination of many things: memory, desires, signs of a language; it is a place of exchange, [...yet,] these exchanges are not just trade in goods, they also involve words, desires, and memories. My book opens and closes with images of happy cities which constantly take shape and then fade away, in the midst of unhappy cities.[16] ('On Invisible Cities' 181)

Although it is said that Calvino was largely inspired by Marco Polo's thirteenth century travelogue Il Milione and Thomas More's Utopia while composing his Invisible Cities, the author himself states that he was not interested in following the footsteps of Marco Polo but in the 'exotic and fantastic stage setting' the traveller had drawn in his Il Milione, the success of which, Calvino asserts, could only be matched with that of A Thousand and One Nights:

---

[16] Taken from the text of a lecture given by Italo Calvino at Columbia University on 29 March 1983; it appeared in Columbia Issue 8.

Only the Thousand and One Nights can boast a similar success – that of an imaginary continent in which other literary works find space for their own particular worlds: continents of the 'elsewhere', now that there is no longer any 'elsewhere' in the world, and the whole world is becoming more and more uniform (and for the worse). ('On Invisible Cities' 179)

In terms of technique, the ingenuity of mathematical design lying behind the author's structural and thematic construction of the work, Invisible Cities is definitely impressive. Invisible Cities is considered to be a postmodern surrealistic representation of fifty-five imaginary cities; however, each of these imaginary cities that bears a female name actually stands for one real city, that is, Venice. According to Abrams, Surrealism emerged as a: '[r]evolt against all restraints on free creativity; included among the restraints to be violated were logical reason, standard morality, social and artistic conventions and norms, and any control over the artistic process by forethought and intention' (Abrams, Glossary 205). The common writerly qualities that could be found in many modern writers of prose and verse, including Italo Calvino, are as follows:

[they] have broken with conventional modes of artistic organization to experiment with free association, a broken syntax, non-logical and non-chronological order, dreamlike and nightmarish sequences, and the juxtaposition of bizarre, shocking, or seemingly unrelated images. (Abrams, Glossary 205)

Likewise, Calvino's book does neither have a beginning, nor a plot, or development of characters in the traditional sense; the author suggests that the reader should first consider the fictional space his book occupies and then read it 'as a book of poems, or essays, or at most short stories' (Calvino, 'On Invisible Cities' 179). The structure of Invisible Cities is based on fifty-five short city descriptions and eighteen dialogues set between Kublai Khan and the Venetian traveller Marco Polo. Concerning Calvino's mathematical orchestration of the book's structure Sophia Psarra writes:

The 55 city descriptions are organised in nine chapters and distributed under 11 thematic rubrics: 'Cities and Memory', 'Cities and Desire', 'Cities and Signs', 'Thin Cities', 'Trading Cities', 'Cities and Eyes', 'Cities and Names', 'Cities and the Dead', 'Cities and Sky', 'Continuous Cities' and 'Hidden Cities'. Each chapter contains five city descriptions (except for the first and last chapters each of which consist of ten cities), arranged so as to construct recursively descending sequences of numbers (from 5 to 1). (Psarra 143–144)

In the book, Polo addresses Kublai Khan, as the 'Emperor of Tartars'.[17] Having sensed the potential destruction of his vast empire, the emperor appoints Polo as ambassador, commands him to visit the distant cities in the far-reaching borders of his empire, and to report back his observations on his return. The emperor's intention is to be truly informed about the physical and practical realities of the cities and of his subjects populating those cities under his rule; thus, by depending on Polo's travel accounts which consist of fantastic city descriptions, and his imaginary experiences of those cities, the emperor seeks ways to consolidate his power and thereby to prevent the downfall of his empire. On the other hand, Robert Ryan's reading of the emperor's pursuit of possessing a centralised sovereign power so as to keep his empire unified is as follows:

> Khan's empire, a presumed totality, receives its orientation from a sovereign power-central presence-that rules from beyond the totality itself; Khan is external to the cities he seeks to possess. In Calvino's language, 'the emperor […] is a foreigner to each of his subjects, and only through foreign eyes and ears could the empire manifest its existence to Kublai'. (Ryan 225)

The 'wise emperor' understands that only a foreigner's external gaze, similar to that of himself, could detect the prevailing problem threatening the unified totality of his empire; and that is the very reason why he appoints Marco Polo as his ambassador.

At the beginning there is a language barrier between Kublai Khan and Marco Polo for the traveller cannot yet speak the native language; therefore, Polo reports his journeys through pantomimes, gestures, exclamations, or through exhibiting various interesting objects:

> Newly arrived and quite ignorant of the languages of the Levant, Marco Polo could express himself only by drawing objects from his baggage – drums, salt fish, necklaces of wart hogs' teeth – and pointing to them with gestures, leaps, cries of wonder or horror, imitating the bay of the jackal, the hoot of the owl.[18] (Calvino, Invisible Cities 38)

---

[17] The historical Kublai, a descendant of Genghis Khan, was Emperor of the Mongols; but in his book (*Il Milione*) Marco Polo referred to him as Great Khan of the Tartars, and thus he has remained in literary tradition (Calvino, 'On Invisible Cities' 179).

[18] The dialogues between Kublai Khan and Marco Polo are italicised in the novel.

Through this inarticulate narrative Polo's imaginary city descriptions take the emperor on a mental journey where one 'could wander through [those cities] in thought, become lost, stop and enjoy the cool air, or run off' (38). At first images make the communication possible between the two; nevertheless, as time goes by, Polo learns the emperor's language, and the emperor starts to understand 'the language of the foreigner'. Thus, images are replaced by words; yet, unlike images, words start to fail Polo in that when the never ending process of recounting every single detail related to those non-existing cities exhausts his imaginative powers, the Venetian traveller '[goes] back to relying on gestures, grimaces and glances' (39). As a silent understanding grows between the emperor and Polo, the communication between the two takes the form of a mute dialogue: '[I]n their conversations, most of the time, they remained silent and immobile' (39). On realising that the cities are mere products of Polo's imagination, the emperor leaves behind his curious inquisitive mood, and asks Marco Polo in an angry tone:

> Your cities do not exist. Perhaps they have never existed. It is sure they will never exist again. Why do you amuse yourself with consolatory fables? I know well that my empire is rotting like a corpse in a swamp…. Why do you not speak to me of this? Why do you lie to the emperor of the Tartars, foreigner? (59)

Having learned the ways to appease the emperor's anger, Marco Polo answers in a calm tone that he is also well aware of the fact that the very foundations of the empire are disintegrating. The Venetian's offered solution which would prevent the empire from falling down is as follows:

> Yes, the empire is sick, and what is worse, it is trying to become accustomed to its sores. This is the aim of my explorations: examining the traces of happiness still to be glimpsed. I gauge its short supply. If you want to know how much darkness there is around you, you must sharpen your eyes, peering at the faint lights in the distance. (59)

In the meantime, the Venetian traveller's insistence on never talking about his native city attracts the emperor's attention and when Polo tells the emperor that he has already recounted all the positive and negative aspects of the cities he visited, the emperor asks the reason why Marco Polo is so discreet about his homeland, why he avoids uttering even the name of his own city. Polo replies: 'Every time I describe a city I am saying something about Venice' (86).

As the emperor's ever dissatisfied hunger for knowledge dictates, he wants to be informed about everything related to Venice – the starting point of Marco Polo's journey to the East. Marco Polo's explanation of his abstinence from describing Venice reads as follows:

> Memory's images, once they are fixed in words, are erased. …Perhaps I am afraid of losing Venice all at once, if I speak of it. Or perhaps, speaking of other cities, I have already lost it, little by little' (87)

Obviously, Marco Polo is afraid of losing the memory of his native city were he to verbalise the dearly kept images of his Venice. The traveller's discretion might be explained with reference to the memory studies. According to the art of memory, while the physical body speaks with words, the soul speaks with images. In fact, body and soul are independent entities; and what connects the body and the soul is called the 'spirit'. Memory and imagination belong to the same part of the soul. Likewise, it is through images that Venice penetrates deep down into Polo's memory and thereby into his soul. Among Polo's imaginary city descriptions 'Cities & Memory - 4' introducing the city named 'Zora' best illustrates the traveller's strategy of storing an indelible vivid image of Venice in his memory. While conversing with the emperor, Marco Polo speaks highly of 'Zora' for he presents it as an unforgettable city. To Polo, those who have seen and memorised all the constituents of Zora are the most learned men in the world. Polo's account of 'Zora' starts with specifying the exact location of the city: 'Beyond six rivers and three mountain ranges rises Zora, a city that no one, having seen it, can forget' (15). In order to memorise his native Venice by heart, Polo follows the strategy of ancient rhetoricians who considered their memories to be an architectural structure, like a palace consisting of such divisions as an anteroom, chambers, halls, hallways, terraces and many others; thus, just like an ancient rhetorician who mastered the art of memory, Marco Polo divides his memory into separate compartments and places in each of those compartments a distinct memory, a scenery, buildings, a fountain, a statue, shops, cafes, a resident of the city, a view of the landscape and the seascape. In doing so, the traveller always remembers the city of his birth no matter how far apart he is. Hence, it is clear that Polo is narrating the life in Venice under the name of 'Zora':

> The man who knows by heart how Zora is made, if he is unable to sleep at night, can imagine he is walking along the streets and he remembers the order by which the copper clock follows the barber's striped awning, then the fountain with the nine jets, the astronomer's glass tower, the melon vendor's kiosk, the statue of the hermit and the lion, the Turkish bath, the cafe at the corner, the alley that leads to the harbor. (15)

Evidently, the attentive reader would immediately recognise that the statues of the hermit and the lion are allusions to Saint Mark, the patron saint of Venice, and to the winged lion, the official symbol of the Venetian Republic; the copper clock is a reference to the Clock Tower in Piazza San Marco; and the astronomer's glass tower signifies the Bell tower of Saint Mark where Galileo introduced his telescope to the Senate of Venice and to the Dodge on 21 August 1609. In addition to the ancient architectural mnemonic, Calvino alludes to the beehive metaphor used by Marco Polo as another memory storage technique while reminiscing about 'Zora':

> This city which cannot be expunged from the mind is like [...] a honey comb in whose cells each of us can place the things he wants to remember: names of famous men, virtues, numbers, vegetable and mineral classifications, dates of battles, constellations, parts of speech. Between each idea and each point of the itinerary an affinity or a contrast can be established, serving as an immediate aid to memory. (15–16)

In a similar vein, in The Book of Memory Mary J. Carruthers discusses some common metaphors like bees and birds or books in a library to maintain an ordered recollection of things:

> Bees and birds (... 'flying things') are also linked by persistent associations with memory and ordered recollection. There is a long-standing chain [..], a texture of metaphor that likens the placement of memory-images in a trained memory to the keeping of birds (especially pigeons) and to the honey-making of bees. [...] And the chain is completed by a metaphoric connection of books in a library both to memories placed in orderly cells and to bird and bees in their celled coops and hives. (35–36)

Thus, it is observed that Calvino's fictional Marco Polo, similar to his historical counterpart, has a trained memory, retaining the 'memory-images' of his native city so vividly that it is as if he were still living in Venice; as if he never left Venice to embark on his adventurous journey 'from Europe to Asia in 1271–95, remaining in China for 17 years'.[19]

'Cities & Eyes - 4', which presents the city named Phyllis, has a distinct place among Marco Polo's descriptions of imaginary cityscapes. Phyllis is one of Calvino's happy cities in that the city has the potential to make the newcomer happy and the departing one feel regretful. Like its actual counterpart, that is, Venice, Phyllis has an enchanting power; the city amazes its residents and visitors with its unique nature as well as with its culture, artefacts, architecture and wealth:

> When you have arrived at Phyllis, you rejoice in observing all the bridges over the canals, each different from the others: cambered, covered, on pillars, on barges, suspended, with tracery balustrades. And what a variety of windows looks down on the streets: Moorish, lancet, pointed surmounted by lunettes or stained-glass roses; how many kinds of pavement cover the ground: cobbles, slabs, gravel, blue and white tiles. (90)

The rich variety of stone and glass works used in the construction of windows, streets and pavements demonstrates that the multi-cultural residents of the fictional Phyllis, which is a mirror reflection of the actual Venice, have a refined sense of aesthetics as well as a considerable wealth. Polo says that every inch of Phyllis is crammed with a wonder amazing the visitor:

> At every point the city offers surprises to your view: a caper bush jutting from the fortress' walls, the statues of three queens on corbels, an onion dome with three smaller onions threaded on the spire. Happy the man who has Phyllis before his eyes each day, and who never ceases seeing the things it contains, you cry, with regret at having to leave the city when you can barely graze it with your glance. (90)

Through this fantastic city, Marco Polo expresses a deep sense of nostalgia he feels for his native Venice, how he longs for his homeland, and how he regrets being away from his city for such a long time. On detecting the regretful tone in Marco Polo's voice, the emperor says,

> It was to slough off a burden of nostalgia that you went so far away!' he exclaimed, or else: 'You return from your voyages with a cargo of regrets!' And he added, sarcastically: 'Meagre purchases, to tell the truth, for a merchant of the Serenissima!. (98)

---

[19] <https://www.britannica.com> 'Marco Polo: Italian Explorer' written by Fosco Maraini, Edward Peters

Regarding Calvino's masterful treatment of multiple city images operating to denote one single city in Invisible Cities Mark Sandy writes:

> Calvino captures the ever-shifting, multifarious nature of the city with his descriptions of multiple fantastical cities, each with their own intrigues, desires, and peculiar spatiality, which are ultimately refractions of a single city: Venice. (205)

In her book titled Venice Variations, Sophia Psarra draws attention to the structural and conceptual analogies between Calvino's book and Venice:

> Both [Invisible Cities and Venice] consist of discrete, small-scale units that are aggregated into networks. The large number of divisible and combinable elements in Calvino's text can be compared to Venice's urban fabric, which consists of discrete islands, buildings and plots which are recursively linked, such as squares, churches, bell towers, wellheads, bridges and loading steps. (170)

Psarra further argues that:

> Both Invisible Cities and Venice have a poly-focal structure and overlapping networks whose organising strength is almost equally distributed into multiple centres. Both have patterns that emerge out of the collective logic of elements, rather than a preconceived idea of a whole. Consisting of a street network and a canal network, Venice is made of one side and obverse, the physical city and its reflection. Further, like Invisible Cities, it has a propensity for doubling and splitting into twin structures.... (170)

Towards the end of his Columbia lecture, Italo Calvino comments on the critics' misinterpretations of the closing sentence of Invisible Cities which reads as follows: 'seek and learn to recognize who and what, in the midst of the inferno, are not inferno, and make them endure, give them space' (165). Since this sentence ends the book, Calvino says, almost every critic assumes it to be the moral of and the conclusion to the novel. However, the author states that his book has not one but many conclusions, depending on each critic's distinct research field and reading of it; the author humbly implies that what causes those ardent controversies whirling around his multifaceted book are the multiple endings that allow the reader to draw inferences according to her/his way of appreciating a postmodern literary text. Calvino exemplifies his point with reference to psychoanalytic critics and to scholars of structural semiology:

> [For instance,] there are psychoanalytic critics who have found the deeper roots
> of the book in Marco Polo's evocations of Venice, his native city, as a return to the
> first archetypes on the memory; while scholars of structural semiology maintain
> that one must seek at the very centre of the book, and by doing so have found an
> image of absence, the city called 'Baucis'. (Calvino, 'On Invisible Cities' 182)

The author's closing remarks underline the text's self-reflexive feature:

> 'Here it becomes clear that the author's view no longer counts; it is as if the book, as
> I have explained, wrote itself, and it is only the text as it stands which can authorize
> or rule this or that reading of it'. (Calvino, 'On Invisible Cities' 182)

In a nutshell, Marco Polo's hometown, Venice, is embedded in all of his fantastic city descriptions in Invisible Cities. The invisible city of the book's title is Venice. Each of the fifty-five seemingly unrelated fictional cities represents a different feature of Venice. All the unreal, presumably improbable fantastic cities are reflections of one real city, which is Venice. As Mark Sandy states, 'For Calvino [...], Venice is the endlessly imagined city and the endless city of imagination' (205). In brief, the book investigates the blurred boundaries between imagination and the imaginable through Marco Polo's reflections on cityscapes.

2.2 Lord Byron's Venice

'Canto IV Venice':

This subsection dwells on George Gordon Byron's, 6th Byron (1788–1824) impressions of Venice as reflected in his 'Canto IV Venice' which is taken from his travelogue titled *Childe Harold's Pilgrimage*. The publication of the first two cantos of *Childe Harold* in 1812 made Byron the best-known English poet of his time. Byron composed the first two cantos while he was on a tour through Spain, Portugal, Albania and Greece, and the cantos cover the poet's city impressions narrated through the voice of a third-person dramatis persona. Byron engaged in composing Canto 3 of *Childe Harold* during another European tour he made through Belgium up the Rhine, then to Switzerland and the Alps. Canto 3 which was published in 1816, was followed by the publication of Canto 4 in 1818, describing the great cities and monuments of Italy. However, it should be noted that although Byron's tour of Italy covers such cities as Arqua, Ferrara, Florence and

Rome, this subsection's specific focus is on Venice only. Byron lived in Venice for three years between 1816 and 1819.[20] During his sojourn in the city he stayed in the Mocenigo Palace located between the Rialto Bridge and Saint Mark's Square. Byron's three-year residence in Venice and the number of works he produced there contributed significantly to the city's worldwide fame and its promotion as a global centre of art and literature; for instance, it was Byron who named the bridge between the Doge's Palace and the prison 'The Bridge of Sighs', turning it into one of the most famous bridges in the world:

> While crossing the bridge linking the Doge's Palace and the prisons, Byron invented the name 'The Bridge of Sighs'-a reference to the imagined sighs of condemned prisoners as they caught a glimpse of Venice for the last time – and so made this one of the best known bridges in the world.[21]

According to David Laven, although Byron, Shelley, Rogers and Moore produced poems on Venice contemporaneously, it was Byron who took the lead in presenting the image of Restoration Venice to the English-speaking world in the nineteenth-century. Laven's account of Byron's domineering role, exceeding those of his contemporaries in introducing the city to the British audience, is as follows:

> The dominant force within this group [, including Shelley, Rogers, and Moore] was undoubtedly Byron himself, in part because he spent over three years more-or-less permanently resident in the city, but also simply because of his unrivalled status as poet of international standing. It was above all through Byron's eyes, or rather through his plays and poems, and then, after his death in Greece, his biographies, that the British public came to know Venice. (Laven 4)

Byron's remarkable poetry as well as his exceptional personality captured the imagination of not only the English-speaking world but also that of the Turkish poet Yahya Kemal Beyatlı, whose poem titled 'Dear İstanbul' is the

---

[20] Lord Byron had grown up in England and Scotland but spent much of his adult life in mainland Europe. He first visited Venice in 1816 and wrote many of his famous works there including parts of the poems *Childe Harold's Pilgrimage* and *Don Juan*. <https://www.nls.uk>

[21] <http://patrickcomerford.com>

first subsection of the following İstanbul section of the present book. Byron's name appears in the opening lines of Beyatlı's poem titled 'Açık Deniz'.[22]

> Balkan şehirlerinde geçerken çocukluğum;
> Her lahza bir alev gibi hasretti duyduğum.
> Kalbimde vardı 'Byron'u bedbaht eden melal
> Gezdim o yaşta dağları, hülyam içinde lal …

The first four lines of the poem convey the profound nostalgia the poet feels for his childhood in the Balkans.[23] The melancholy tone accompanying Beyatlı's dreamlike journeys back into his childhood is quite similar to Byron's melancholy portrayal of Venice.

Coming back to Byron's Venice experiences, David Laven also states that he is as much interested in discovering the literary nature of the relationship Byron sets between himself and Venice, and how the poet presents his systematically distorted vision of the city, as the number and the literary merit of works Byron produced in and about Venice:

> [Byron's] Ode on Venice, Canto IV of Childe Harold's Pilgrimage, his comic experiment with ottava rima, the humorous Beppo, and his two historic plays – Marino Faliero and The Two Foscari – written in Ravenna after he departed the former Serenissima, represented the city and its past, but it strikes me as important both to stress the essentially literary nature of Byron's relationship with Venice, and to highlight the extent to which he systematically distorted perceptions of it. (4)

Added to the works mentioned in the previous quotation, Byron also composed his Don Juan, though partly, in Venice.

Regarding the influence of Byron's close friend, John Cam Hobhouse, on the creation process of Canto 4, Andrew Rutherford writes:

---

22 The poem 'Açık Deniz' does not have an English translation, but the English translation of the title might be 'The Open Sea'.

23 Yahya Kemal Beyatlı was born in Skopje (now in Macedonia). Beyatlı studied in Paris for several years and subsequently taught at İstanbul University. After the proclamation of the Turkish Republic, he held several ambassadorial posts. Although he supported republican principles, much of his poetry glorifies the Ottoman past. His lasting artistic achievement was his synthesis of classical Ottoman and French poetry. <https://www.britannica.com>

> The fourth canto of Childe Harold's Pilgrimage was dedicated to John Cam
> Hobhouse, who had shared many of the Italian experiences it commemorated.
> The two men had travelled from Switzerland to Venice in October-November 1816;
> [...] they had spent five happy months together at La Mira or Venice, while Byron
> added a large number of stanzas to his first draft of this canto. He was glad to have
> his friend's congenial company and to benefit by his erudition, while Hobhouse
> [enjoyed] having thus been present at the conception and birth parts of the new
> poem. (Rutherford 391)

Prior to the discussion on Canto 4, it might be helpful to dwell on the formal
structure of the work. Childe Harold is a narrative poem written in cantos.
Canto is defined as a subdivision or part in a narrative or epic poem, consisting of stanzas with five or more lines each. Lord Byron structured his
long poems Childe Harold's Pilgrimage (1812) and Don Juan (1819–1824) in
cantos.[24] Byron wrote all the cantos of Childe Harold in Spenserian stanzas,
consisting of eight iambic pentameter lines followed by one iambic hexameter
(an Alexandrine), rhyming ababbcbcc. (Abrams, Glossary 200). In the first
canto, following the model of his eighteenth-century predecessors, Byron
imitated, in a seriocomic fashion, the archaic language of the Elizabethans;
for instance, the word 'Childe' is the ancient term for a young noble awaiting
knighthood. But he gave up the archaisms, and in the last two cantos he
adapts Spenser's sweet-sounding stanza to his own assured and thundering
high-flown language (Abrams, Glossary 491). In the preface to his first two
cantos, Byron stated that the narrator, Childe Harold, was a fictitious character; yet in the fourth canto, the poet abandoned the third-person dramatis
persona and spoke out in the first-person. Concerning Byron's replacement
of the third-person narrator, Childe Harold, by a first-person narrator in
Canto 4, James L. Hill in 'Experiments in the Narrative of Consciousness:
Byron, Wordsworth, and Childe Harold cantos 3 and 4' states that while
Childe Harold appears to become a shadow figure in Canto 3, '[...] by Canto
4 he has virtually disappeared, leaving the subjective Byronic consciousness
in possession of the rest of the poem' (121). The reason for this shift might be
the readers' insistence on identifying the character as well as the travels of the
protagonist with those of the author. Childe Harold owes its distinguished

---

[24] <https://www.britannica.com/topic/Childe-Harolds-Pilgrimage>

place in English poetry to its composer's style, consisting of apostrophes, imperatives, exclamations, hyperbole and abrupt changes in subject, pace and mood. Byron ingeniously transformed a tourist's record of scenes, monuments, art works, and museums into a dramatic and passionate experience. The poem, Childe Harold, is regarded as an expression of melancholy and disillusionment due to the Post-Revolution and Napoleonic eras (Abrams, Norton 491). In Mark Sandy's words, Venice in Canto 4 is 'a place of rich promise and possibilities worthy of preserving for posterity, but it is equally a force already spent, fallen into physical and political ruin' (210). According to the scholar, Byron was inspired by William Wordsworth's 'Ode: Intimations of Immortality' while composing Canto IV of Childe Harold's Pilgrimage in that the poet associates the rise and fall of Italian history and culture, that of Rome and Venice in particular, with Wordsworth's portrayal of man's fall from 'celestial light' into the 'light of common day' (209). Byron's melancholy tone is apparent in the following lines where the poet observes the ruins of a great civilisation:

> The commonwealth of kings, the men of
> Rome!
> And even since, and now, fair Italy!
> Thou art the garden of the world, the
> home
> Of all Art yields, and Nature can decree;
> Even in thy desart, what is like to thee?
> Thy very weeds are beautiful, thy waste
> More rich than other climes' fertility;
> Thy wreck a glory, and thy ruin graced
> With an immaculate charm which can not
> Be defaced.[25]

However, while lamenting over the remnants of the Roman and Venetian ruins, Byron still captures the traces of an indelible grace rising over 'the wreck' of a once glorious civilisation: 'Recalling mankind's fall in Eden, Byron finds in Roman and Venetian decline an oxymoronic "ruined grace"

---

[25] <https://knarf.english.upenn.edu/Byron/charold4.html>

and remnants of a "glory" in the "wreck" of this civilisation' (Sandy 210). Considering Byron's feelings stimulated by the beauty of this 'wreckage' one cannot help reminiscing Yahya Kemal and Tanpınar wandering around the poor quarters of İstanbul in the first decades of the twentieth century. Just like Byron, the two Turkish authors found in the old, impoverished neighbourhoods of İstanbul a wreckage not to be mourned after but a timeless beauty and perfection created and destroyed by various civilisations. In that case, the three poets' similar sentiments evoked by the ruins of great civilisations approve the Freudian idea that contrary to the transience of political power, the notion of beauty is everlasting. The portrayal of Venice as a sinking beauty and its glorious past as a dying one as well as Byron's lamenting tone appear to be a recurrent theme in the opening lines of Ode on Venice[26] which was published in 1819. The following lines of the lyric express a profound sense of sadness Byron feels on witnessing a decaying, decadent Venice. In line 5, the poet presents himself as a foreigner, 'a northern wanderer' shedding tears of helplessness before the presence of Venice, the magnificent mercurial city gradually sinking into the depths of the Adriatic Sea; the magical city is returning to the waters which once gave birth to it. The sight of the submerged Venice would merge the tears of the Venetians as well as those of the foreigners with the 'sweeping' waters of the Adriatic Sea. If a foreigner like himself feels so sad, Byron states, the Venetians must have been much sadder for their vanishing city:

Oh Venice! Venice! when thy marble walls
Are level with waters, there shall be
A cry of nations o'er thy sunken halls,
A loud lament along the sweeping sea!
If I, a northern wanderer, weep for thee,
What should thy sons do? -anything but weep:
And yet they only murmur in their sleep.[27]

---

[26] 'A long lyric poem that is serious in subject and treatment, elevated in style and elaborate in its stanzaic structure' (Abrams, *Glossary* 137). Please see Appendix B for the full text of the poem.

[27] The excerpt is taken from <https://www.best-poems.net>

Byron's four stanzas opening 'Canto 4 Venice' reflect similar sentiments:

I
I stood in Venice on the Bridge of Sighs;
A palace and a prison on each hand:
I saw from out the wave her structures rise
As from the stroke of the enchanter's wand:
A thousand years their cloudy wings expand
Around me, and a dying glory smiles
O'er the far times, when many a subject land
Look'd to the winged Lion's marble piles,
Where Venice sate in state, throned on her hundred isles!

II
She looks a sea Cybele, fresh from ocean,
Rising with her tiara of proud towers
At airy distance, with majestic motion,
A ruler of the waters and their powers:
And such she was; – her daughters had their dowers
From spoils of nations, and the exhaustless East
Pour'd in her lap all gems in sparkling showers.
In purple was she robed, and of her feast
Monarchs partook, and deem'd their dignity increased.

III
In Venice Tasso's echoes are no more,
And silent rows the songless gondolier;
Her palaces are crumbling to the shore,
And music meets not always now the ear;
Those days are gone – but Beauty still is here.
States fall, arts fade–but Nature doth not die,
Nor yet forget how Venice once was dear,
The pleasant place of all festivity,
The revel of the earth, the masque of Italy!

IV
But unto us she hath a spell beyond
Her name in story, and her long array
Of mighty shadows, whose dim forms despond
Above the dogeless city's vanish'd sway;
Ours is a trophy which will not decay
With the Rialto; Shylock and the Moor,
And Pierre, cannot be swept or worn away –
The keystones of the arch! Though all were o'er,
For us repeopled were the solitary shore. (508–509)

The first stanza presents Byron as the speaker of the canto. The poet is standing on the Bridge of Sighs with the Doge's Palace on his left and the prison of San Marco on his right. In the speaker's eyes, Venice is a magical city born out of the Adriatic Sea. The city casts its spell on the visitors like an enchanter. The patron saint of Venice is Saint Mark; some of his relics are kept in Venice, at St Mark's Basilica. His emblem, the winged lion, was erected on a huge marble pillar. Saint Mark's lion is a symbol of the city's magnificence and power. The speaker refers to the many isles and to the glorious history of Venice but calls that glory a 'dying' one implying that Venice is no longer the richest and the most powerful city state of the Mediterranean region and its victorious past has vanished long ago.

In the second stanza, Venice is likened to Cybele, a nature goddess who is presented with a 'tiara', a crown on her head. Likewise, Venice is called the 'Queen of Adriatic' or else 'La Serenissima'. The city has a majestic air for it dominated the entire Mediterranean region with its naval forces for centuries. The city was wealthy because all the riches of the East showered over Venice thanks to its past status (fifteenth and sixteenth centuries) as the leading maritime power. Nevertheless, the glory and the imperial dignity of the city vanished when Napoleon Bonaparte invaded Venice in 1797. The city is personified and depicted as an aristocratic woman dressed in a 'purple robe'. The symbolic significance of the colour purple is that it is often associated with royalty, rarity, piety, magic, and mystery; obviously, Byron ascribes all these sublime characteristics to Venice.

In the third stanza, the speaker is saying that it is not possible to hear gondoliers' voice singing Tasso's 'Jerusalem Delivered'[28] anymore. The gondoliers are rowing silently without chanting. The splendid palaces are crumbling. The glittering resplendent days of Venice are gone, but the city is still beautiful because natural beauty is everlasting. Powerful states might fall, or artworks and artists might be forgotten, but the majestic memory of Venice, its unique natural beauty can never be forgotten. The city has been and is still a centre

---

[28] La Gerusalemme liberata (Jerusalem delivered) is an epic poem by the late Renaissance Italian poet Torquato Tasso (1544–1595). Written in the eight-line stanzas common to Italian Renaissance poetry, Tasso's masterpiece is known for the beauty of its language, profound expressions of emotion and concern for historical accuracy. The subject of the poem is the First Crusade of 1096–1099 and the quest by the Frankish Knight Godfrey of Bouillon to liberate the sepulchre of Jesus Christ. Library of Congress (.gov) <https://www.loc.gov>.

of joy and festivity with its carnivals and miscellaneous artistic activities throughout centuries. It is noteworthy that Byron replaces his lamenting tone by a note of hope, or a strong belief in the future of Venice that the city would revive and recapture the glory of the bygone days.

In the last stanza, the poet underlines the enduring power of literature in keeping the unmatched sight of Venice always unspoilt, fresh and alive in the collective memory. Here, Byron speaks on behalf of literary giants. The poet's claim is that contrary to the transient glory of rulers, the trophy of authors would immortalise the beauty of Venice in their works. The reference is made to William Shakespeare's *Merchant of Venice* and *Othello* as well as to Thomas Otway's *Venice Preserved*. In all these three plays Rialto, the business district in Venice, is used as the setting. In an interview, the Turkish author Nedim Gürsel remarks how challenging it has always been for him to write anything on Venice, not due to the city's rich history or its unique topography, but rather due to the overwhelming number of the great literary masters, such as Musset, Pushkin, Byron, Mann, Hemingway, Proust, and Calvino, who had already written on the subject.

As for Hobhouse's alleged role and influence on the composition process of 'Canto IV Venice', Andrew Rutherford ends his article by saying that Hobhouse's contribution to the work is undeniable, for 'he did present Byron with a list of objects' to be used in the poem. However, as Byron's letters to friends and acquaintances proved, Hobhouse's list played a minor part in the composition of Canto IV. To put it simply, Rutherford claims, Canto IV owes its success to its creator alone. Rutherford's final remarks on Byron's poetic genius read as follows:

> Hobhouse's part in the composition of Canto IV was much smaller than he himself imagined, or than later readers have surmised. The selection of topics for poetic treatment was almost entirely Byron's own work, and the subject matter and main emphases of this poem are the result, not of Hobhouse's influence, but of Byron's own recent experiences and interests, and the nature of the material which Italy provided. (Rutherford 397)

The similarity of the sensory impressions Venice leaves on the two authors – the former being an Italian, and the latter an English man – is noteworthy in that both authors were inspired by and attracted to the magical beauty of Venice, and both pictured the very special topography of the cityscape according to their distinct authorial preferences. While Italo Calvino fictionalised a historical figure, the thirteenth-century traveller Marco Polo, to narrate a surrealistic representation of Venice in his postmodern novel, in his Romantic poem it is Lord Byron himself commenting on the everlasting beauty of the city, despite the fact that Venice's glorious status as the most powerful city state of the Mediterranean region was a thing of the past. Thus, despite the generic, stylistic, temporal, ideological and even national differences between the two authors, the urban landscape evoked in both Calvino and Byron could be expressed in one single word: adoration. Regarding the fading glory of once powerful states, Rimbaud's representation of London in his prose poem, 'The Bridges', where the poet alludes to the weakened status of British imperialism, might be given as a final example.

The following subsection explores Venice from the perspective of Henry James as reflected in his *Italian Hours*. Henry James's *Italian Hours* is a travelogue, a collection which includes the author's essays on Italy. The work is classified as a brilliant example of classic non-fiction.

2.3 Henry James's Venice

> Venice has been painted and described many thousands of times, and of all the cities of the world is the easiest to visit without going there. Open the first book and you will find a rhapsody about it … (James 1)

Until the publication of Washington Irving's, *The Sketch Book of Geoffrey Crayon, Gent.* (1819–1920)[29] writing travel accounts came to be seen as an outworn mode of literary production. However, the success of Irving's *Sketch Book* convinced the nineteenth century 'educated readers and aspiring writers' [including Henry James] that 'sketching' Europe presented a challenging test of literary talent' (Pauly 108). Literary sketch is a 'short prose narrative, often an entertaining account of some aspect of a culture written by someone within that culture for readers outside of it'. Its style is informal, and compared to the tale and short story, it is less dramatic but more analytic

---

[29] Washington Irving used the pseudonym Geoffrey Crayon for the first time for this travelogue.

and descriptive.[30] Thus, following the model of Washington Irving's *Sketch Book*, which is an account of the English landscape and customs for readers in the United States, Henry James (1843–1916) published his impressions of Italy in his travel sketches titled *Italian Hours*, which he penned between 1872 and 1909, and this subsection of the book engages in the American modernist author's critical perception and representation of the image of Venice as the old aesthetic urban space whose organic beauty is attacked by modernity under the name of improvement. The author 'visited Italy almost annually for about forty years' (Mariani 239). At the age of twenty-six, the young promising author set foot in Italy for the first time in 1869. Robert L. Gale in his article titled 'Henry James and Italy' portrays the contradictory feelings Italy evokes in the young author as follows:

> [James] first descended upon Italy in September, 1869, and not only was the youth of twenty-six enthralled on his road to Rome by way of Venice and Florence – for here were paintings, buildings, statues, cities, ruins and scenery almost beyond his dreams – but he was also puzzled. (157)

The Italian nature, culture and works of art impressed James so deeply that he regretted for being late to discover such an enchanting country. Robert Gale describes the author's mood on his first encounter with Italy as 'enthralled', and in a euphemistic way, 'puzzled'. In fact, as Robert L. Clair suggests, James was not puzzled but felt angry with his parents: 'Why had his parents never taken him to this wondrous land during the several trips the entire cosmopolitan and deliberately rootless family made?' (Clair quoted in Gale 158) James' intention in writing *Italian Hours* was to convey to the American audience his physical and cerebral experience of Italy, of Venice in particular, through his highly refined modernist style. Thus, James' passion for travelling, his interest in and knowledge of the art of painting, the inspiration he drew from Irving's *Sketch Book*, accompanied by his desire to depict the picturesque in prose, engendered Italian Hours. Regarding the influence of the travel sketch on Irving and James, Thomas H. Pauly writes:

> …both [Irving and James] celebrated the sketch for its conceptual, rather than representational, rendering of experience…. The travel sketch, which was for them a prose account, was considered a similar exercise of the artistic sensibility in the

---

[30] <https://www.britannica.com/art/literary-sketch>

act of appreciation; it arose from the same desire to involve the mind in the eye's delights. (109)

Obviously to James, possessing a painter's vision is of primary importance for a writer because without such a gift he/she could not transfer images into words; the painterly eye, to James, enables the writer to distinguish between what is pictorial and what is not. In that respect, the young critic James was deeply impressed by the travel descriptions of the French writer Théophile Gautier whom James believed to have been gifted with such a painterly vision. In James's words:

Gautier was blessed with a perception of material beauty so intense and comprehensive that he was unable to write five lines without creating a lovely image or ministering in some odd fashion to the delight of the eyes … he was blessed with an actual relish for the pictorial. (James quoted in Pauly, 111)

As is seen, drawing picturesque images in words is dependent on the author's ability to establish an aesthetic correlation between the perceiving mind and the gazing eye. It is understood that James was concerned with framing images in words while recounting his travel experiences. Evidently, to succeed in doing this one ought to have not just the gift to write but a painterly vision, and undoubtedly, James had both.

In her article titled 'We have botched them and patched them: Modernity and Restoration in Henry James's *Italian Hours*', Monica Manolescu-Oancea focuses on Henry James's reflections on modernity and its vulgar tasteless impact on the Italian cityscape. To Manolescu-Oancea, the process of restoration, which was regarded as an agency of modernity, became a controversial issue among the intellectual and artistic circles of the nineteenth-century. Henry James was among the ones who were irritated, even 'horrified by the results of restorations in Italy, for reasons having to do with his vision of the organic growth of buildings, with his stance as a discreet and uninvestigating traveller and with his criticism of improvement as bad taste' (2). Indeed, in the opening of Venice section of the *Italian Hours*, James frankly voices his preference for the old and his distaste towards any kind of novelty that he sees as the intrusion of modernity which irreparably harms the organic bond among the edifices, Venetians and the very special exquisite nature of Venice; to put it briefly, there is no room for the new in Venice. The author holds the view that,

> …for the true Venice-lover Venice is always in order. There is nothing new to be said about her certainly, but the old is better than any novelty. It would be a sad day indeed when there should be something new to say. (James 1)

It is observed that the author's reflections upon Venice are replete with an intense feeling of melancholy; for James, '[Venice] is a city in which there must be almost as much happiness as misery' (3). The city's melancholy image manifests itself as the urban space which is sad and joyous simultaneously. To James, this paradoxical idea of being sad and cheerful at the same time might be traced in the mood of Venetians as well. The author relates the Venetians' mercurial and melancholy mood to a number of advantages and disadvantages: as for the disadvantages, 'Their habitations are decayed; their taxes heavy; their pockets light; their opportunities few' (3); yet, despite the hardships Venetians have to tackle, the American author claims, 'It takes a great deal to make a successful American, but to make a happy Venetian takes only a handful of quick sensibility' (3). In the eyes of James, the cityscape provides Venetians with an exceptional spectacle with its generous nature, with the streets embellished with magnificent works of art by great artists; such an atmosphere to the author not only heightens the Venetian sensibility, but also that of 'the sentimental tourist who is gratified by the sight of a beautiful race that lives by the aid of its imagination' (3). In brief, according to James, Venetians lead a happy, peaceful life granted to them by the mild Mediterranean climate and nature; together with their fellow citizens, they experience and enjoy an unmatched aesthetic physical space created by the hands of various artists who produced their works of art and monuments in Venice for Venetians throughout centuries.

For a foreigner to fully grasp and internalise the organic bond between the Venetian cityscape and the Venetians, James says, what must be done is to stay in Venice for a long time, and to treat her with great care and affection like a beloved woman: 'The only way to care for Venice as she deserves it is to give her a chance to touch you often| – to linger and remain and return' (4). The author's use of the pronoun 'she' while referring to Venice displays that he attributes female features to the city. This idea of gendering the cities in question is interesting; for instance, London is identified sometimes as gender fluid (or having an androgynous identity), and sometimes as having masculine traits; on the other hand, İstanbul, like Venice, is almost always depicted as a woman whose enchanting and everlasting beauty has kept inspiring authors/ poets and artists for ages.

Henry James's nineteenth-century Venice, which he described as a unique open-museum piece, evokes the same contradictory feelings even in the present-day tourist in that the spectacle of the city sometimes falls short of masking its defected spots from the keen-eyed visitor. The author divides visitors into four groups: the ordinary ones and the sentimental ones; and those who like and who dislike being in Venice; and then proceeds to recounting the flaws that make the sentimental tourist find the city as 'odious':

> The Venice of to-day is a vast museum where the little wicket that admits you is perpetually turning and creaking, and you march through the institution with a herd of fellow-gazers. There is nothing left to discover or describe, and originality of attitude is completely impossible. This is often very annoying; you can only turn your back on your impertinent playfellow and curse his want of delicacy. (5)

Nevertheless, the author puts the blame not on the city but on the rest of the world for its imperfections. For instance, James holds responsible those tourist crowds and likens them to barbarians who attack the city like reckless plunderers looting the cultural, architectural, and natural beauties of Venice:

> The barbarians are in full possession and you tremble for what they may do. You are reminded from the moment of your arrival that Venice scarcely exist anymore as a city at all; that she exists only as a battered peep-show and bazaar. There was a horde of savage Germans encamped in the Piazza, and they filled the Ducal Palace and the Academy with their uproar. The English and Americans came a little later. They came in good time with a great many French, who were discreet enough to make very long repasts at the Caffé Quadri, during which they were out of the way. (7)

It is noteworthy that James's critique of the boisterous tourist herd is directed mainly at the Continentals: the insensitive shallow ones are the Germans and the French. Evidently, he speaks in favour of his fellow Americans and the English. (There is no doubt that Henry James would have been much more irritated had he lived in Venice and witnessed present-day tourist hordes visiting the city from all around the world).

Venice might lose its initial charm in the eyes of those whom the author calls 'the shallow inquirers' if their sojourn in the city exceeds one week; they might find the typical tourist excursions around the ancient monuments, piazzas, palaces, bridges, the Grand Canal and other water-ways, gondoliers and gondola tours, the importunate Venetian street vendors – recently replaced by immigrants from all around the world – and the malodorous shallow lagoon as monotonous, nasty, and boring. On such occasions, the city turns out to be a tourist trap; she drops her mask and exhibits her rotten decaying face to the tired tourists. Consequently, such a tedious experience urges the 'shallow inquirers' to a quick departure. In that case, the author says, the loss would be not of Venice but of the unsentimental shallow visitors departing from the city, unaware of the things they missed; how they missed the chance of having such a rich and once-in-a-lifetime experience. According to James, such visitors are the most disagreeable things in Venice.

However, what must the foreigner do for a true appreciation of this very exquisite cityscape? The author's response is clear: to experience Venice in 'a responsible and intelligent manner' (4) and treat the city with great care. At that point the author's Venice image, personified as a beautiful but difficult woman reappears on the stage. The author's (admittedly male-centred and heteronormative) advice to the foreign visitor is that "he" should assume the role of a sentimental, passionate and faithful lover whose only goal is to win a place in the heart of the dearly loved woman and to remain there eternally. The author states that this is the only way to establish an everlasting bond between the foreigner and Venice; also, the longer the foreigner stays in Venice, the stronger and more permanent the bond would be:

> It is by living there from day to day that you feel the fullness of her charm; that you invite her exquisite influence to sink into your spirit. The creature varies like a nervous woman, whom you know only when you know all the aspects of her beauty. She has high spirits or low, she is pale or red, grey or pink, cold or warm, fresh or wan, according to the weather or the hour. She is always interesting and almost always sad; but she has a thousand occasional graces and is always liable to happy accidents. (6)

As is understood, once the foreigners are united with the city spiritually, they would be granted all the wonders that Venice could offer to non-Venetians; in addition, they would be loved and cherished in the way they deserve. Thereby, Venice becomes a much-desired lover:

> The place seems to personify itself, to become human and sentient and conscious of your affection. You desire to embrace it, to caress it, to possess it; and finally a soft sense of possession grows up and your visit becomes a perpetual love affair. (6–7)

Another issue that bothers James as much as the hordes of tourists is the never-ending construction and restoration work of the Italians, which not only interferes with the appreciation of the city's historic texture but also gravely harms the organic bond between the Venetians and the city's ruins that constitute the city's very special architectural heritage. Although the said goal of restoration seems to be logical and convincing, that is to protect the ancient architectural heritage against potential natural and temporal damages, and transmit it unharmed to future generations, the author ardently suggests that the city's very special edifices and ruins should remain untouched. Thus, James approaches this ambiguous process of incessant restoration in a melancholy mood and ponders upon the matter: What makes Venice look so feeble, so decrepit? The author could not decide whether it is the outcome of a tasteless style of restoration, or the existing decrepitude of the monumental structures that makes the style, which James calls 'inveterate', seem so vulgar: 'Is it the style that has brought about the decrepitude, or the decrepitude that has, as it were, intensified and consecrated the style?' (64) The author then turns his eyes to the enigmatic city ruins that create the oxymoronic attraction of the Venetian decay. According to Manolescu-Oancea, 'Venetian ruins (actually all the ruins of Italy) are perfect, [...] complete and unsurpassable in their apparently fragmentary state – a paradoxically holistic fragment' (4). Likewise, to James, since it is the sense of melancholy rising over the fragments of ruins that bestows the Venetian urban space its unmatched beauty, they should definitely remain untouched. Based on John Ruskin's view of the early Venetians, who were exiles from ancient and beautiful cities and had been accustomed to build with their ruins Manolescu-Oancea claims that 'Ruins as a foundation become ruins as a destiny, the inevitable fragmentary condition of a city whose architecture had already incorporated fragments into its organic development' (4).

As for the tawdry effects modernity brought about on Venice, Henry James first focuses on the vulgar, clingy pedlars who are invading and tainting the spiritual atmosphere of the whole Piazza district, that of St Mark's in particular, while trying to sell their useless cheap wares:

> I had chiefly in mind the impression that assails me to-day in the whole precinct
> of St Mark's. The condition of this ancient sanctuary is surely a great scandal. The
> pedlars and commissioners ply their trade [...] at the very door of the temple; they
> follow you across the threshold, into the sacred dusk, and pull your sleeve, and
> hiss into your ear, scuffling with each other for customers. There is a great deal of
> dishonour about St Mark's altogether, and if Venice, as I say, has become a great
> bazaar, this exquisite edifice is now the biggest booth. (James 7–8)

As is seen, the author's complaints are not limited to the exterior of the
cathedral in that after depicting the disrespectful vendors disrupting the
sacred air surrounding the ancient edifice, James turns his critical painterly
eye to the interior of the building, to the restorer whose work, says the author,
destroyed the beauty of the interior once and for all: 'Wherever the hand
of the restorer has been laid all semblance of beauty has vanished; which
is a sad fact, considering that the external loveliness of St Mark's has been
for ages less impressive only than that of the still comparatively uninjured
interior' (8). The author asserts that restorers and pedlars are equally responsible for demolishing the original beauty of St Mark's, based on the edifice's
centuries long organic connection with the Venetian landscape, climate and
the Venetians. To the author, it is the restorer's hand that stroke the final
blow to the cathedral's relatively less damaged interior: 'The old softness and
mellowness of colour – the work of the quiet centuries and of the breath of
the salt sea – is giving way to large crude patches of new material which have
the effect of a monstrous malady rather than of a restoration to health' (8).
The ultimate result of the restoration process, as exemplified in detail by
referring to that of St Mark's, is voiced by James as, 'Dear old Venice has
lost her complexion, her figure, her reputation, her self-respect; and yet, with
it all, has so puzzlingly not lost a shred of her distinction' (64). Indeed, the
following quote best expresses how James regards the ongoing process of
restoration works in Venice as a series of betrayals committed for so-called
'improvement': 'We have botched them and covered them with sordid signs;
we have restored and improved them with a merciless taste...' (37).

Nevertheless, it is observed that James's cynicism is replaced by an intense
feeling of appreciation and adoration when he is describing the Ducal Palace:[31]

---

[31] When the Doge's Palace was built, it had a design similar to a castle, with towers in
the corners as it was in a strategic point of access to the sea. From this Palace, 120

'This deeply original building is of course the loveliest thing in Venice, and a morning's stroll there is a wonderful illumination' (22–23). The author's emphasis on the word 'original' is noteworthy in that James is likely to be alluding to the building's state of being yet untouched by the hand of the restorer. To James, the best hour to enjoy this wonderful building is 1 pm, for it is the time when the sun beams and the sea light from the glittering lagoon fuse to play light games on the walls and ceilings of the Ducal Palace; consequently, the author says, 'All the history of Venice, all its splendid stately past, glows around you…' (23). The author then assumes the role of an art critic and proceeds to make comments on Paolo Veronese's painting titled 'The Rape of Europa'[32]. James's evaluation of the painting also includes his suppositions on the temperament of the artist which he describes as elevated, exuberant and happy:

> [Veronese] was the happiest of painters and produced the happiest picture in the world. 'The Rape of Europa' surely deserves this title; it is impossible to look at it without aching envy. Nowhere else in art is such a temperament revealed; never did inclination and opportunity combine to express such enjoyment. The mixture of flowers and gems and brocade, of blooming flesh and shining sea and waving groves, of youth, health, movement, desire – all this is the brightest vision that ever descended upon the soul of a painter. Happy the artist who could entertain such a vision; happy the artist who could paint it as the masterpiece I here recall is painted. (23–24)

According to Thomas H. Pauly, Henry James's interest in paintings and illustrations stimulated by his desire to find order and coherence in the outside world initially enabled him to excel 'in the domain of art criticism, where he refined that intellectual grasp of painting which subsequently proved as essential to his writings on travel as it was to his seminal essay on 'The Art of the Novel" (111). The rich figurative language and refined style James employed while expressing his evaluation and adoration of the paintings of the great Renaissance artists like Titian, Tintoretto and Veronese, who are

---

doges directed the fate of Venice for almost 1000 years. The building is regarded as a masterpiece of Gothic architecture. One distinguished quality of the building is that its colour changes depending on the time of the day; the building acquires a very delicate pink tonality always keeping in the symmetrical gothic gives a pinkish with White colour. The ducal palace Venice <https://www.venice-museum.com>.

[32] Paolo Veronese (1528–1588) was one of the major painters of the sixteenth-century Venetian school.

also called 'The Venetian Trio',[33] and the Bellini family,[34] confirm Pauly's claim that the author's deep attraction to the art of painting, his eagerness to have a painter's eye contributed much to his professional writing career. Thus, *Italian Hours* became the site, rather the canvas upon which the young Henry James painted his visual and sensual experience of the Italian art and landscape, sharing it with his American audience.

To Umberto Mariani, the young Henry James's early impressions of Italy, based on the myth of a romantic Italy and thereby etched to his visual memory, were mainly shaped by his readings on the great Romantic writers:

> With Byron and Shelley, Hawthorne and Ruskin, Stendhal, George Sand, Chateaubriand, and Mme de Staél as his literary guides, Italy took for James the stock romantic form of a 'dishevelled nymph', country of genius and dirt, of lovely – and false – people, heirs of imperial glory and Renaissance lustre, still capable of Emperors' cruelties and Borgia intrigues; a country where precious opportunities for initiation into the arts […] were still waiting for the American thirsty for beauty and the past. And from the fascination of the lyric opera, with its fabulous pictorial settings, the exaggerated glory of its singers, the romantic adventures of its plots, the myth receive a final touch. (238–239)

For Mariani, this romantic myth of Italy created by the author's adolescent imagination evolved into maturity and 'gained new vitality' only as late as the last decades of the visits he paid to the country. According to Mariani, while one of the reasons for the delay is James's negation of having a realistic contact with the changing circumstances of the country and its local people, the other ones are his stubborn loyalty to his mythicised vision of Italy, accompanied by his unchanging stance as an outsider. To Mariani, Henry James did not step outside the lines drawn by his romantic vision of Italy for a long span of time; the critic related the author's intentional

---

33 Despite the rivalry among them, these three painters of the Renaissance Venice influenced and inspired one another. Their contribution to artistic revival was huge in their use of oil on canvas; their focus on colour as opposed to line and the emergence of easel painting that was to transform not only Venetian art but also the whole of European painting itself. <https://mini-site.louvre.fr>

34 The Bellini family of painters was one of the most influential names in the Italian Renaissance. Jacopo Bellini (1396–1470), Giovanni's father, was a leading painter at the start of the Renaissance. Jacopo's two sons, Giovanni (1430–1516) and Gentile (1429–1507), carried on this immense influence, with Giovanni carrying great importance in the Venetian style of painting. <https://www.virtualuffizi.com>

belatedness in facing the new realities and recording the changing socio-cultural dynamics in Italy to James's adherence to his alien stance, especially towards the Italians. As Mariani states, James kept himself aloof from the Italian cultural and political circles: '[James] does not seem to have looked very far for a means of comprehending the Italian people, having neglected the usual means of knowing the people of a country; familiarity either with them or their literature' (242).

Thus, the author preferred to recount his experience of the nature, culture, art, music, and architecture of Italian cities, including Venice, from the outsider's perspective. In a sense, his literary ends urged James to keep a distance between himself and the Italian people. He deliberately avoided establishing an authentic emotional contact with the Italians for a long time. Nevertheless, the unavoidable change in James's notion of the idealised romantic Italy finally started to burgeon in his style and in his themes as the author's sojourn in the country prolonged:

> With time, his Italian landscapes ceased to be merely a picturesque backdrop for romantic adventure and were endowed with some of the richness of symbolic values inherited from great historical events. The inflated exclamations gave way to more accurate [realistic] writing; new essays were written to correct earlier judgements and impressions; and James ultimately became a master in interpreting the foreign traveller's reaction to the Italian landscape. (Mariani 242)

It is observed that James left behind his alien identity as soon as he faced and accepted the new realities brought about by modernity. Regarding the influence of Venice on his personal life and authorship, James writes:

> It was a charming time; one of those things that don't repeat themselves; I seemed to myself to grow young again. The lovely Venetian spring came and went, and brought with it an infinitude of impressions, of delightful hours. I became passionately fond of the place, of the life, of the people, of the habits. … I lodged on the Riva, 8…] The view from my windows was una bellezza; the far-shining lagoon, the pink walls of San Giorgio, the downward curve of the Riva, the distant islands, the movement of the quay, the gondolas in profile. Here, I wrote diligently every day and finished, or virtually finished, my novel. (James quoted in Gale 161)

Upon hearing the enchanting siren-like voice of Venice, James, then the mature author, could not keep himself from visiting the city for two weeks for the last time. James defined those two weeks he spent in Venice as divine. Evidently, Venice as the urban landscape not only nourished and enriched the artist's soul but also instilled in him an immense desire for a joyous life of artistic productivity. Considering the multitudinous number of the author's works either composed, or finished, and/or set in Venice, the reader fully grasps what Venice meant to Henry James, and why he associated his happiest and most prolific times as a writer with that particular city. As Robert L. Gale states, 28 of James's 135 short stories and novels are cast entirely or partly in Italy:

> The Portrait of a Lady, started in Florence in 1880, was finished in Venice a year later. Several essays, for example 'The Grand Canal' (1892) and 'Casa Alvisi' (1902), concerned admired spots there. A few stories were conceived, and others written, there. [...] For two examples among more, 'A London Life' (1888) was begun in a Venetian palace, [...] as its preface tells us, while the short novel The Reverberator (1888) grew from the notoriety attaching to a tactless American woman's exposure of Venetian society manners in a letter to a New York newspaper. (162)

A final remark might be made on the connection between this present section on Henry James's Venice and the following section of this book, which is devoted to two Turkish authors' works on İstanbul: not only Henry James but also both Yahya Kemal Beyatlı and Ahmet Hamdi Tanpınar owe much to Théophile Gautier regarding the construction of the city image in their narratives. The French author's unique ability to detect the pictorial among the commonplace, vapid, nasty, or even the wrecked, and to create exquisite images out of it inspired the above-mentioned authors while composing their works on the urban landscape. Concerning Gautier's keen eyes, his distinctive perceptual capacity that enabled the French Romantic author to draw images and pictures in words, Henry James writes: '[Gautier] sees pictures, where most people find mere dead surfaces, and where common eyes find the hint of a picture he constructs a complete work of art' (James quoted in Pauly 112). To conclude, all three of the said authors borrowed their gift of expressing the picturesque in words from Gautier, following in Gautier's footsteps in depicting these two peculiar cities, Venice and Istanbul, through the discerning and refined vision of a painter.

İstanbul

Whenever I find myself talking of the beauty and the poetry of the Bosphorus and
Istanbul's dark streets, a voice inside me warns against exaggeration, a tendency
perhaps motivated by a wish not to acknowledge the lack of beauty in my own life.
If I see my city as beautiful and bewitching, then my life must be so too.
—PAMUK (50)

The cityscape to be explored in this last chapter is İstanbul. İstanbul, with
a history spanning 8500 years, with its singular geography located at the
intersection of the two Continents – Asia and Europe – and with its rich
cultural heritage embodying the remnants of many ancient civilisations,
is regarded as a unique urban landscape as Venice, undoubtedly. Since the
Middle Ages, İstanbul has been thought of as a city of contradictions, diver-
sity, and complexity; the cityscape still preserves the said characteristics in
the twenty-first century. In the book titled *Constantinople byzantine et les
voyageurs du levant* Jean Ebersolt notes that İstanbul has always played a major
role as a bridge connecting Eastern and Western civilisations. According to
Ebersolt, the overlapping cultural heritage of Greek, Roman, Byzantine,
and Turkish civilisations, 'created this bizarre and sorrowful, exciting and
mysterious city, …' (6).

The Turkish poets/authors to be investigated respectively in this last chapter
are Yahya Kemal Beyatlı (1884–1958), Ahmet Hamdi Tanpınar (1901–1961)
and Orhan Veli Kanık (1914–1950). The reason for the selection of three
works, namely 'From Another Hill', the 'İstanbul' section of *Five Cities*, and
'I am Listening to İstanbul' by these three Turkish authors is that all of them
convey their authors' common feelings of love of and a deep commitment to

the city they lived in. For instance, during the first years of the foundation of the young Turkish Republic, Yahya Kemal Beyatlı and Ahmet Hamdi Tanpınar created an indigenous İstanbul image combining the beautiful with the bizarre, the miserable and the sordid, which gives way to a sense of melancholy rising over the ruins of a collapsed empire (The Ottoman empire). The reader might also note that the imprints of a certain amount of nostalgia, a lamenting tone, or aspiration felt for the glorious days of the past, accompany the image of İstanbul in all the three works. Concerning the vanished magnificence of a cityscape, it is also observed that Lord Byron's treatment of Venice and the three Turkish authors' attitude towards İstanbul definitely bear affinities. Also, the keen reader might undoubtedly notice a similar melancholy tone in the Venice narratives of Lord Byron and Henry James, and those of the Turkish poets'/author's works dedicated to İstanbul. A delicate sensitivity towards natural beauties of the urban landscape could be detected in both Wordsworth's 'Composed upon Westminster Bridge' and Orhan Veli's 'I am Listening to İstanbul', and the speakers in both said poems have similar stances while pondering upon the defining characteristics of the two different cities -- London and Istanbul, respectively. On the other hand, an awareness of the social condition of underprivileged working-classes is reflected powerfully in Blake's 'London' poem, while it is only slightly touched upon in the works of Ahmet Hamdi Tanpınar and Orhan Veli Kanık.

3.1 Yahya Kemal Beyatli's İstanbul

Yahya Kemal Beyatlı, bearing such titles as the 'supreme craftsman', or 'the greatest of İstanbul poets', wrote poems of love, nostalgia for the Ottoman past, the beauties of İstanbul and the metaphysics of life and death through a highly refined and melodious language. To Abide Doğan, on reading the works on Paris by Mallarme, Verlaine, and Baudelaire, Yahya Kemal decided to write poems on İstanbul, the city which the poet thought deserved commemoration through poetry more than Paris. Abide Doğan's[35] account of Yahya Kemal's İstanbul, what the city meant to the poet might be translated as follows:

---

[35] Doğan, Abide. 'Yahya Kemal'in İstanbul'u'. <https://dergipark.org.tr>

To Yahya Kemal, İstanbul was the epitome of the homeland. İstanbul was the city reflecting the collective spirit that built the nation. After the foundation of the Republic of Türkiye, İstanbul was not the political capital anymore but became the site wherein the national spirit was shaped and propagated. It was İstanbul that not only enriched and refined the Turkish sense of aesthetics but also solidified the Turkish will; hence, the Turkish language as well as ways of living gained elegance. The poet integrated such concepts as culture, civilisation, history, homeland, geography, arts, religion, nation and national identity with İstanbul in his poems. ('Yahya Kemal'in İstanbul'u' 167)[36]

The poem, 'From Another Hill'[37] is one of the best poems reflecting the poet's deep attachment to and love of İstanbul. It is a short poem consisting of two quatrains, and it is written in 'aruz' metre. And, like Byron in 'Canto IV Venice', Yahya Kemal himself is the first-person speaker in the poem. The poem is as follows:

'From Another Hill'[38]
I looked at you from another hill, dear İstanbul!
I know you like back of my hand, and love you dearly
Come, come and sit on my heart's throne as long as I live
Just to love a district of yours is worth a whole life.

There are many flourishing cities in the world.
But you're the only one who creates enchanting beauty.
I say, he who has lived happily, in the longest dream,
Is he who spent his life in you, died in you, and was buried in you.[39]

The poem is an elaborate expression of Yahya Kemal's love of the city wherein the poet confesses not to have disliked any neighbourhood that he has visited.[40] By the way, it is worth to note that Yahya Kemal was born in Skopje,

---

[36] I translated the quotes I took from Abide Doğan's article, ['Yahya Kemal's Istanbul'] from Turkish into English.

[37] Please see Appendix C for the full original Turkish text of the poem.

[38] The poem was made into a song by the famous Turkish composer Münir Nurettin Selçuk.

[39] Translated into English by Ümit Yaşar Oğuzcan 10 Favourite Poems for Istanbul. <https://www.weloveist.com>

[40] Yahya Kemal Beyatlı's and Ahmet Hamdi Tanpınar's İstanbul excursions are partly drawn from my article titled 'Orhan Pamuk's İstanbul Carved in his Memory as a Source of Melancholy'.

and he came to İstanbul in 1902 for the first time when he was eighteen; he spent a year in a relative's house (İbrahim Bey's), and a year later in 1903, he left İstanbul for Paris where he lived for nine years (Doğan 165). Coming back to the first quatrain, the poet declares loudly that no other city could replace İstanbul which is the only city that he will love until the end of his life. Yahya Kemal asserts in the poem that knowing intimately even one single neighbourhood of the city is such a rich and fulfilling experience that equals a lifetime. In the second quatrain, İstanbul appears to be the only city possessing enchanting beauties. Interestingly, however, Venice is also said to have the same characteristic in both Calvino's *Invisible Cities* and in Byron's 'Canto IV Venice'. Another common point detected between the city descriptions of Calvino and Yahya Kemal is that both authors portray Venice and İstanbul as happy cities capable of making their residents happy; also, in the works of both writers the two cities are depicted as forces that trigger the authors' imagination, and ultimately as sites of poetic creation because the writers of these two iconic cities embraced and dearly loved them – even in their weakest and most devastated states. Furthermore, the historical significance attributed to İstanbul as the city of cities might be found not just in the entirety of Yahya Kemal's poetry, but in the pages of the atlas owned by Calvino's great khan, Kublai in Invisible Cities. Calvino combines history and myth while recounting İstanbul's role in the foundation of great cities created by various civilisations. While leafing through the pages of Kublai's atlas, which maps all the past, present, and future cities in the world, Marco Polo notices that unlike such ancient cities as Jericho, Ur, and Carthage, Troy did not disappear after the Greek attack and invasion of the city, but evolved first into İstanbul – then called 'Constantinople' – in 1453, and ultimately 'from the mixture of those two cities a third emerged', (Calvino, Invisible Cities 138) said Calvino, in the shape of the present-day San Francisco. In the book, Marco Polo's reading of this mythical transformation of Troy into 'Constantinople', the conquest of the city by Mehmed II, the seventh of the Ottoman sultans, who would later be given the epithet 'the conqueror' is as follows:

> But speaking of Troy, he happened to give the city the form of Constantinople and foresee the siege which Mohammed would lay for long months until, astute as Ulysses, he had his ships drawn at night up the streams from the Bosporus to the Golden Horn, skirting Pera and Galata. (Invisible Cities 138)

As is seen Calvino treats Troy and İstanbul as the two archetypical cities; the author's association of Mehmed II with the Homeric epic hero Ulysses as well as his choice of words while narrating the siege of the Byzantine Constantinople by the Ottoman Turks clearly indicate that Calvino appreciates the military genius lying behind the conquest of the city. Likewise, in Yahya Kemal's poetry, İstanbul is the epitome of a glorious past and the emblematic city of the young Turkish Republic. It is İstanbul wherein the poet grounds his notion of homeland. Obviously, Yahya Kemal takes pride in İstanbul's history, a theme that can be traced in the majority of his poems.

Yahya Kemal considers a life spent in İstanbul to be dreamlike. Particularly, the last two lines of the poem indicate the poet's two different treatments of time spent in İstanbul, the city of enchanting beauties. Martin Stokes in his 'Three Versions of Beloved İstanbul' interprets the presence of two kinds of time in the poem as follows: 'One might perceive a tension in the poem between two different kinds of time, one is an orderly historical progress in which love begins, develops, and reaches maturity and repose after long experience. The other kind of time is a stepping out of time, as if into a dream – a significantly more unstable prospect' (159). In fact, the first stanza of Yahya Kemal's poem, 'Verses to Bedri'[41] might be regarded as the epitome of the poet's love for İstanbul. In the said stanza, the poet says, 'If I had a chance to return from the afterlife, to be reborn, and were I even to be invited by fate, most politely, to choose any star I please as my stately residence in the sky, I would still, still wish to return to İstanbul'.

Scholar Yusuf Eradam ingeniously recounts why he is so deeply attached to and in love with İstanbul in his 'autobiographically inspired (and non-academic)' essay titled 'My Sense of Belonging to İstanbul'. The author personifies the city as a dearly missed woman, a protective mother, and a muse who has kept inspiring his artistic creativity by nurturing his sense of aesthetics even during his long years of absence from İstanbul. The following quote reflects how the author overcame the lack of parental care and affection in

---

[41]   The Turkish original of the stanza is as follows:
'Bedri'ye Mısralar' / Gelmek'çün ikinci bir hayata, / Bir gün dönüş olsa ahretten; / Her ruh açılıp da kâinata, / Keyfince semada bulsa mesken; / Talih bana dönse nazikâne; / Bir yıldızı verse malikâne; / Bigâne kalır o iltifata, / İstanbul'a dönmek isterim ben.

the boarding school days of his childhood; the solution he found was to replace the love of his absentee parents with the city:

> Starting from a personal history, loss of family (especially the love of parents) and childhood for the sake of some good education at a boarding school in İstanbul, the child's need is to transfer that lack of the love of the parents to the love of a metropolis. After eight years of good education, I had to live and work in Ankara for 33 years missing İstanbul, my first beloved. It is also about how I looked forward to retirement from Ankara University in 2004, when I quickly signed the papers and flew to my 'woman' (my polis), to my lands of creativity and freedom, a landscape that opened when I arrived in İstanbul at the age of eleven. (51)

The author's last sentence describing how fast he 'flew' to İstanbul is very much reminiscent of Robert Herrick's lines dedicated to London which I used as the epigraph opening the London chapter of this book. In the following long quotation, Eradam explains how passionately he feels as one with İstanbul, and how this sense of belonging is inalterable and unexchangeable:

> The sense of belonging for a person who has chosen to live there does not mean to go to the touristic attractions like the highlights of the historic peninsula, The Topkapı Palace, or Hagia Sophia, or the Covered Bazaar, the Blue Mosque. I made another song in which I express my wish to die in one of the bays of this beautiful city, a wish as an outcome of the fact that I think I know I am part of some transcendental big whole when I am here, in İstanbul. It is some instinct, some incurably, hopelessly romantic feeling that I am; that I know I exist when I know I will die, as Edward Albee also underlines. I want to die here İstanbul, though I had the chance to spend the rest of my life and die in Las Vegas, Michigan, New York of the USA; London or Edinburgh of the UK; Rome, Venice of Italy, and Vienna of Austria. (56–57)

On reading about the author's wish to live, die, and be buried in İstanbul, one cannot help recalling especially the last two lines of Yahya Kemal's 'From Another Hill': 'I say, he who has lived happily, in the longest dream, / Is he who spent his life in you, died in you, and was buried in you'.

3.2 Ahmet Hamdi Tanpınar's İstanbul

Ahmet Hamdi Tanpınar's 'İstanbul' is a prose work taken from the collection titled *Five Cities* which recounts the author's observations and experiences of the five cities, namely Ankara, Erzurum, Konya, Bursa and İstanbul. The book was first published in 1946. The İstanbul section of Tanpınar's *Five Cities* is accepted as one of the rare sources written about life in İstanbul in the past as well as in the first half of the twentieth century. The author's detailed observations and realistic descriptions inform the reader about the climate, the urban landscape, architecture, culture, social structure, multifarious lifestyles, and the literary, artistic and intellectual history of the city. Tanpınar's reflections on the past and present of the city prove that he was overwhelmed by nostalgic feelings. In the opening of the İstanbul section, the author refers to the miraculous healing power of the city's spring waters by recalling a childhood memory. The author and his father met an old woman who invented a magic method of recovery when she was afflicted with high fever. According to the son-in-law of that old woman, his mother managed to reduce her body temperature by simply reciting the names of İstanbul's spring waters, 'Çırçır, Karakulak, Şifa, Taşdelen, Sırmakeş...' (115) like an enchantress performing an act of incantation. The son-in-law explained the process of her quick recovery:

> As these names squeezed through her taut, dry lips and under her tongue that was heavy as molten lead, her lustreless eyes came to life, her whole face grew attentive as though she was listening to things inaudible to us and her hollow cheeks filled out with concentration. [...] It's her medicine, it works like a charm... as she tells over the names she begins to recover. (115)

It is observed that Tanpınar gives specific importance to İstanbul's flora. For instance, he refers to cypresses and plane trees as leaving unforgettable marks in the collective memory of the city:

> The overall view of the city, [...] owes much to the cypress groves like those at Karacaahmet, [...and] Edirnekapı. Some views gather around the plane trees in those atmospheric spiritual corners of the Bosphorus, and the cypresses of Eyüp once gave the whole of the Golden Horn its character. (157)

Tanpınar puts particular emphasis on the fir tree and the stone pine as these two trees have a remarkable role in the construction of İstanbul's melancholy image: 'We owe the authentic melancholy of İstanbul's land and seascape to two trees, the fir tree and the stone pine, both of which play a large part in developing our emotional sensibility' (157). Tanpınar then expresses a deep sadness for İstanbul's vanishing greenery. Along with the modernisation process of the twentieth century, İstanbul lost a substantial amount of its groves and woods. The author equates the loss of a tree with the fall of a monument or of a great work of art. To the author, nothing can recompense the death of a centennial tree:

> Gradually İstanbul is losing her trees: it is not like our losing some old custom or tradition. Traditions vanish because others succeed them, or because they are no longer necessary, but the disappearance of a centuries-old tree is a different matter. Even if another tree is planted in its place it requires time to influence the landscape. And if it eventually succeeds, it cannot be the same tree blessed by our forefathers when they lived beneath it. (157)

According to Tanpınar, history, culture, nature, architecture and the inhabitants of İstanbul are so tightly interwoven that the loss of even one single tree weakens the emotional ties of a nation based on centuries:

> The death of a tree is like the loss of a great work of architecture. Sadly, and inevitably, for a century or even more, we have become used to the loss of both. One after another, before our very eyes, masterpieces crumble into a heap of dust and ashes like a heap of salt that has fallen into the water. (157–158)

The author then calls attention to the deplorable condition of İstanbul's architectural heritage, and to the ruined state of its monumental buildings which need urgent restoration. Tanpınar likens the ruined scenery of the city to a terminally ill patient who is on the verge of death. Here, a parallel might be drawn between Tanpınar's metaphor displaying a ruined İstanbul in the first half of the twentieth century and that of William Cobbett presenting the nineteenth-century Industrial London as a malignant tumour defiling the evergreen image of rural England:

> [A]ll over İstanbul, in every quarter, there are columns toppled, roofs collapsed, old religious colleges full of rubbish and charming little neighbourhood mosques and fountains in ruins. It would take little effort to restore them, but they deteriorate a bit more every day. They lie prone on the ground like the dead in an epidemic whom the living has not the strength to remove. The day that we realise that true creativity begins with preserving what already exists will make us happy. (158)

Tanpınar thoughtfully warns that İstanbul will keep losing its historical, architectural, and cultural heritage unless serious measures are taken to preserve them. Here, the author calls for an urgent need for a holistic approach and an expert insight to restore the crumbling monumental structures of İstanbul, thus taking the opposite point of view from what Henry James, to recall, most feverishly defends in the "Venice" section of his *Italian Hours.*

Tanpınar continues to discuss the peculiar characteristics that make İstanbul an iconic city. Monumental mosques like the Blue Mosque built by 'Sedefkar Mehmet Ağa' who was a disciple of the great architect Sinan, the old mansions on the shores of the Bosphorus, İstanbul's indigenous street vendors, and even the awkward habits of the inhabitants such as watching the famous İstanbul fires are among some of the details related to life in İstanbul. The author openly expresses his discontent of the changing ways of living in İstanbul along with the modernisation attempts of the Republican Era:

> Today's neighbourhood is not as it once was, an organic community closely bound by strong ties, but is simply a section of municipality. The neighbourhood has gradually been replaced by a high-rise block of flats, a little tower of Babel where a different radio station blares from every window, the inmates ignorant of who live above or below, indifferent to the living or the dead. (Tanpınar 129)

It is observed that Tanpınar also complains about the weakened human contact along with the urbanisation accelerated with modernisation. The close ties and warm feelings of neighbourhood culture prevailing in the old İstanbul disappeared in a short span of time. In 'İstanbul as Poetic Space via the Works of Turkish and British Writers", Medine Sivri and Başak Özker investigate the concept of the city as the poetic space of intimacy, memories and dreams with reference to Gaston Bachelard's book titled *The Poetics of Space.* Bachelard's theory on the cityscape focuses on the intertwined connection of space, memory and time. As Sivri and Özker state, Bachelard defines his concept of space 'as topophilia and his aim as examining the images of the felicitous space and to reveal the human value of these spaces that are owned, defended and loved' (262). Based on Bachelard's idea of the role and importance of spaces of happiness in the literary production, Sivri and Özker explain the reason why İstanbul as the poetic space has been inspiring the memorable works of Turkish as well as foreign authors: 'The fact that İstanbul is handled by many local and foreign authors is an indication of the city's poetic structure that activates memories, imagination and dreaming' (262). The 'İstanbul' section of Tanpınar's *Five Cities*, Halide Edib Adıvar's *House with Wisteria* and *The Turkish Ordeal*, Samiha Ayverdi's *İstanbul Geceleri* and Orhan Pamuk's *İstanbul Memories and the City* are among the works included in the article by Sivri and Özker. The two authors note that the common point in the selected works of their Turkish writers' 'memories and experiences of İstanbul contain intense longing for the previous years that the authors spent in the city. Although, the [said] authors wrote their works on different dates, the period in which each of them focused with longing and intense emotions is the 'past', which they identify with happiness' (263). Tanpınar's regretful melancholy tone in the following quote indicates that the old İstanbul as the space of happiness has fallen into oblivion together with its nature, architecture, intimate neighbourhood culture and with its true inhabitants, whom the author sees as 'the real poets of İstanbul':

> Today, the neighbourhoods are no more. Only scattered here and there throughout the city are some old, poverty-stricken former inhabitants, old inhabitants who endure countless difficulties as they wander from district to district, sometimes emerging from hidden corners to ask news of each other, to drink their coffees and recall the past. For me, they are the real poets of İstanbul. (Tanpınar 128–129)

Evidently, in Tanpınar's eyes, the image of the old İstanbul as the poetic space of happiness activating memories, imagination and dreaming has become a thing of the past; Tanpınar's contemporary İstanbul has lost its aesthetic and poetic charm, its exquisite capacity to inspire and stimulate the creative skills of authors/poets, and artists because the organic bond between the city and its old inhabitants has been irretrievably damaged due to the changes brought about by the modernisation process of the twentieth century.

The author then proceeds to compare the old and present style of İstanbul's coffee houses to those he experienced in Vienna. The unchanging style of coffee houses in Vienna leads him to ponder upon the present condition of those in İstanbul, and the conclusion he draws is that the furnishing of the cafes 'with the arrival of tables and chairs' first changed the scenery and then, the spirit of the old coffee houses in İstanbul:

> On the morning after my first night in Vienna, […] I took breakfast in the Mozart Café and was amazed when the waiter placed before me a pile of newspapers, just as in the İstanbul coffee houses of my youth. The Viennese still persisted in a style we had borrowed from them. (169)

Tanpınar's profound admiration for the unchanging spirit of Mozart Café essentially stems from the establishment's capacity to deliver to its patrons a timeless aesthetic sensory experience, similar to the impact of Mozart's music on the audience. Tanpınar cherishes the idea that, notwithstanding the inevitability of change, it is necessary to respect and preserve those characteristics of a literary work, a musical composition, or a building that make them timelessly beautiful. The author observes that, while the musical (semai) coffee houses of İstanbul underwent physical renovations during the large-scale modernisation efforts of the Republic era, they regrettably lost most of their authentic spirit as venues that had been known in the past to nourish their patrons as well as their frequenters both culturally and intellectually through recitals of music and poetry.

Also, Tanpınar makes comments on the history of the teahouses as the public spaces that contributed much to brighten up the social life in İstanbul. Along with the modernisation attempts of the Ottoman Empire during and after the 'Tanzimat'[42] period, the first teahouses appeared in 'Beyoğlu' (the district was then called 'Pera') in the reigns of Selim III and Mahmud II in the nineteenth-century; leading the Tanzimat were Mahmut's sons, Abdülmecit I (1839–1861) and Abdülaziz (1861–1876). The author likens those teahouses to the present time little cafes he saw in Italy and Spain. However, the difference Tanpınar mentions is that İstanbul's teahouses served only men:

> İstanbul gentlemen used to watch women taking their evening stroll, especially during Ramazan, just as they now do, sitting on the café terraces in Madrid and Seville; but at that time, they watched from behind glass. The evening stroll (which the people of İstanbul named the passegiata, after the Italian) was one way to enliven the old city of İstanbul after the Tanzimat period. (170)

Another interesting habit attributed to both the foreigners and the Muslim residents of the nineteenth-century İstanbul was the cemetery excursions. Especially, during the reign of Abdülmecit I, the multi-religious inhabitants

---

[42] The Tanzimat-i Hayriye or 'Auspcious reorderings', was a period of sustained legislation and reform that modernised Ottoman state and society, contributed to the further centralisation of administration, and brought increased state participation in Ottoman society between 1838 and 1876. <https://www.cambridge.org>

of İstanbul took walks in the shady pathways of diverse sizes of cemeteries that were surrounded by many cafes:

> In the early years of Abdülmecit's reign, [...] Muslims as well as Christians, and women in particular, often walked in the cemeteries, which were a little beyond the regular walkways and were regarded as city gardens. (170)

Tanpınar describes the trajectories of those promenades in detail and adds that one could easily visualise those neighbourhoods, cemeteries, cafes, and the social life of the nineteenth-century İstanbul by either reading the İstanbul section of Nerval's Voyage en Orient[43] (Voyage to the East), or by seeing the engravings of Melling[44] or Allom.[45] Tanpınar refers to Gautier's reflections on the freedom zone of women living in the nineteenth-century İstanbul, and says that contrary to the common belief, Turkish women were not living behind bars, and theirs was not a life confined to the narrow space of a 'harem': 'Gautier says they were not so deprived of freedom, as was generally thought, but were at liberty to walk, provided they were accompanied by the eunuchs who supervised the harem' (170).

The book also includes the author's personal accounts of the significant life-changing coincidences he experienced while living in those cities; hence, the book is considered to be much more than an ordinary travelogue. Undoubtedly, the discussion on Tanpınar's 'İstanbul' should go in parallel with the way Yahya Kemal Beyatlı perceived the city in that Tanpınar was both student and a life-long friend of 'the greatest of İstanbul poets'. Yahya Kemal's İstanbul image has a profound impact on Tanpınar's representation of İstanbul. Having been influenced by the two French authors – Gérard de Nerval and Theophile Gautier – the two Turkish authors attached the word 'melancholy', which would later be replaced by its Turkish equivalent 'hüzün',

---

43 Gérard de Nerval (1808–1855) was a French Romantic poet whose themes and preoccupations influenced the Symbolists and Surrealists. 'Nerval's journey to the Orient had a literary end: to regain the respect of his peers, to re-create himself thriugh the construction of a vastly complicated literary tour de force. Nerval's goal was to follow his imagination, his dreams, and his illusions of the Orient to their very limit, in order to accomplish his literary work and renew himself in literature' ('Orientations: Writing the Self in Nerval's *Voyage en Orient* 66).

44 Please see Appendix E for the biography of Antione Ignace Melling (1763–1831).

45 Please see Appendix F for the biography of Thomas Allom (1804–1872).

to their İstanbul image. The two melancholy authors particularly wandered around the poor neighbourhoods of İstanbul searching for inspiration that would feed their literary needs and creative skills. Contrary to Byron, who felt a deep sense of awe in the presence of the magnificent rich scenery of Venice, what enchanted the two Turkish 'flaneurs' were İstanbul's ruins they saw during the excursions they made to the poor quarters of the city in the early twentieth century. This ruined scenery played a complementary role in the two authors' melancholy image of İstanbul to which they added the senses of loss and defeat. In *İstanbul Memories and the City*, Orhan Pamuk quotes Tanpınar's 'A Stroll Through the City's Poor Neighbourhoods' to display how the author perceives İstanbul's beauty and symbolic significance:

> 'I see the adventures of these ruined neighbourhoods as symbolic. Only time and sharp shocks of history can give a neighbourhood such a face. How many conquests, how many defeats, how many miseries did its people have to suffer to create the scene before us?'. (Tanpınar quoted in Pamuk 224)

It is observed that here Tanpınar's melancholy is not a subjective sentiment generated by pondering on the defeats and/or conquests that mark the lifetime of one or more civilisations. It rather stems from witnessing the presence and the overwhelming flow of time in the materialised form of these ruins. The author's melancholy mood resulting from the ruined scenery before his eyes confirms Fatih Aydoğan's comment on the function of Tanpınar's intertwined use of space and time in the work: 'Tanpınar initially views the city as a space; then reminisces the historical figures lived within the cityscape. For him, space and history (time) are intertwined. The author views the city from a vantage point. He takes shelter in historical monuments, and occasionally, delves into his own solitude' (31). In Tanpınar's case, the memory of the city, the recollection of the past lives lived in İstanbul, the remnants of old civilisations appease his melancholy feelings; Calvino's fictitious Marco Polo, however, hides the memory of his homeland deep down in his subconscious; he even avoids uttering the name of the city in order to keep the vision of his beloved Venice forever alive in his memory; this act of never mentioning Venice also helps the traveller to ease the sense of homesickness to some extent.

Regarding the type of melancholy experienced by Tanpınar and Yahya Kemal, and Peter Schwenger's description of melancholy which the writer associated with physical objects, bear remarkable resemblances. In his introduction to *The Tears of Things: Melancholy and Physical Objects* Schwenger distinguishes two types of melancholy: the first one is the traditional lament for the ephemeral object, and the second is the one that is produced 'by the act of the perception of the object by the subject' (2). Schwenger claims that: '[this moment of] perception, always falling short of full possession, gives rise to a melancholy that is felt by the subject, and is ultimately for the subject. It is we who are to be lamented, and not the objects that evoke this emotion in us without ever feeling it themselves' (2). Hence, it is understood that on seeing the ruins of a collapsed empire before their eyes, the two Turkish authors mourn not for the transient objects but for themselves, and more accurately in a metonymic mode, for the Turkish nation.

The dream-time experienced by the two Turkish authors in İstanbul might be compared to that of Calvino's Marco Polo who could imagine himself living in Venice only in his dreams as he could not return to his homeland for twenty-four years. According to Stokes, for those who experienced the city in a dream-time, the urban landscape 'became the locus of a distinct phantasmagoria, approached via dream, fantasy, [and] reminiscence …' (5). The difference between the two Turkish authors and Calvino's Marco Polo is that while the former two are experiencing a dream-time city during their residence in İstanbul, the latter imagines a dream-time Venice while he is living in the Far East. This dream-time experienced by the two melancholy Turkish authors in İstanbul might be better understood with reference to Kristeva's *Black Sun*. To Kristeva, in terms of spatio-temporal relations, a melancholy mind's perception of time is distorted. Time does not flow; it is immobile and fixed upon a certain moment or period, a certain space, and a certain memory: '… massive weighty, doubtless traumatic because laden with too much sorrow or too much joy, […] a moment blocks the horizon of depressive temporality or rather removes any horizon, any perspective' (60). Thus, certain moments of time and place fixate the melancholy mind to either a great joy or a great sorrow. Kristeva then refers to Kant to emphasise depression's reliance on time rather than place: 'Considering the specific variant of depression constituted by nostalgia, Kant asserted that nostalgic persons did not desire the place of their youth but their youth itself' (Kant qtd in *Black Sun* 60). Hence, it is understood that the two Turkish authors cherished the desire to return to a dream-time İstanbul instilled in their memory. Evidently, neither the pains of World War I, nor the turbulent days of the new Republican Era could distort the melancholy beauty of İstanbul image in the memory of the two authors of the city.

The connection between melancholy and the ability of finding beauty in the ruined, impoverished quarters of İstanbul where the two Turkish authors persistently walk and witness the wreckage of three successive empires might be explained with reference to two essays by Freud, both published in the last years of World War I. In 'On Transience', Freud defends the everlasting quality of beauty. Contrary to the common belief in the transient and hence sorrowful nature of beauty, Freud claims in the essay that the notion of beauty is defined not by transience but by endurance. Paradoxically, beauty is not only resistant to temporal limitation but also immune to every kind of material damages like those caused by wars or natural disasters. What is considered to be beautiful and perfect may undergo material damage or even vanish entirely; yet material damage or loss neither diminishes the value of the beautiful object nor changes the way it was and is still remembered. Hence, the conclusion Freud draws is that 'our high opinion of the riches of civilisation has lost nothing from our discovery of their fragility' (307). Likewise, what Yahya Kemal and Tanpınar saw in İstanbul in the first decades of the twentieth century was not a wreckage to be mourned but a timeless beauty and perfection created and destroyed by various civilisations. Freud's 'Mourning and Melancholia' also sheds light on why those İstanbul walks were accompanied by melancholy. As Freud remarks, melancholy differs from mourning in that it is characterised by a feeling of self-reproach resulting from the loss of the loved object. However, this kind of self-reproach, guilt, or responsibility for the lost object is absent in mourning (244). The scenery of the 'old and bizarre' İstanbul makes the two authors directly experience man's power to create as well as to destroy great civilisations. This experience inspires a simultaneous exaltation and sorrow, the former for the majestic works that man is capable of, and the latter for the fragility of such works. When a sense of responsibility is adjoined to the sorrow in the face of destruction, as in the case of Yahya Kemal Beyatlı and Ahmet Hamdi Tanpınar, melancholy is born.

3.3 Orhan Veli Kanık's İstanbul

Orhan Veli Kanık (1914-1950) is the last poet whose intimate ties with İstanbul will be discussed herein. Compared to the previously mentioned two Turkish authors, Orhan Veli was younger. Despite his short life of only thirty-six years, he produced 'a substantial body of work, which includes five books of poetry, essays on poetry and literature, short stories, radio plays, topical writing for newspapers and magazines' (Erol 398). Together with his friends, Oktay Rıfat and Melih Cevdet Anday, Orhan Veli founded a literary movement called the 'Garip'. Concerning the content of 'The Garip Manifesto' which was written by Orhan Veli himself for their volume of poetry titled *Garip* (1941), Sibel Erol writes:

> [Garip] has a familiar feel to those versed in the modernist movements of other poetic cultures. It vehemently decries rhyme, metre, and rhetorical devices like metaphors and similes as artificial conventions. It undertakes to find musicality in the rhythms of everyday speech, address the working class, and mine the unconscious through dreams and desires in order to achieve sincerity and authenticity. The first volume was sold with a band around the book that said 'You will be questioning everything you know'. (398)

As is noted in the previous quotation, Orhan Veli was an innovator, a true reformist who rejected the conventions of earlier Turkish poetry, and the selected poem, 'I am Listening to İstanbul' is one of the poet's best exemplifying not only the structural and stylistic innovations Orhan Veli brought to Turkish poetry but also his deep love of İstanbul. Talat Halman's English translation (1982)[46] of the poem is as follows:

'I am Listening to İstanbul'

I am listening to İstanbul, intent, my eyes closed;
At first there blows a gentle breeze
And the leaves on the trees
Softly flutter or sway;
Out there, far away,
The bells of water carriers incessantly ring;
I am listening to İstanbul, intent, my eyes closed.

I am listening to İstanbul, intent, my eyes closed;
Then suddenly birds fly by,

---

46 <Turkishclass.com/poem_193> Please see Appendix D for the Turkish original of the full text of the poem.

Flocks of birds, high up, in a hue and cry
While nets are drawn in the fishing grounds
And a woman's feet begin to dabble in the water.
I am listening to İstanbul, intent, my eyes closed.

I am listening to İstanbul, intent, my eyes closed;
The Grand Bazaar is serene and cool,
A hubbub at the hub of the market,
Mosque yards are brimful of pigeons,
At the docks while hammers bang and clang
Spring winds bear the smell of sweat;
I am listening to İstanbul, intent, my eyes closed.

I am listening to İstanbul, intent, my eyes closed;
Still giddy since bygone bacchanals,
A seaside mansion with dingy boathouses is fast asleep,
Amid the din and drone of southern winds, reposed.
I am listening to İstanbul, intent, my eyes closed.

I am listening to İstanbul, intent, my eyes closed;
Now a dainty girl walks by on the sidewalk:
Cusswords, tunes and songs, malapert remarks;
Something falls on the ground out of her hand,
It's a rose I guess.
I am listening to İstanbul, intent, my eyes closed.

I am listening to İstanbul, intent, my eyes closed;
A bird flutters round your skirt;
I know your brow is moist with sweat
And your lips are wet.
A silver moon rises beyond the pine trees:
I can sense it all in your heart's throbbing.
I am listening to İstanbul, intent, my eyes closed.

This long poem by Orhan Veli depicts İstanbul in Spring. It is written in free verse; the language is plain and colloquial. The persona is seemingly meditating upon the natural beauties of İstanbul. He appears to be in a state of absolute tranquillity, and this stance of the persona is reminiscent of Wordsworth's speaker pondering upon the early morning scenery of the silently sleeping London. Nevertheless, Orhan Veli's urban landscape is not silent; the persona of the poem is "listening" to the sounds, sights, odours, and the various activities of the inhabitants. The line 'I am listening to İstanbul, intent, my eyes closed' opening and ending each stanza is used to emphasise that the persona does not need eyes to see the beauties of the city. In the poem, the ears of the persona fulfil the function of the eyes, and this act of experiencing one sense in terms of another indicates that Orhan Veli's synesthetic perception of the city recalls Rimbaud's impressionistic view of London in 'The Bridges'. The İstanbul images in the poem are stimulated, visualised, and conveyed to the audience by the persona's auditory sense. The poetic persona could hear, smell, and touch the city even though he might be physically away from the city. İstanbul has such a distinguished place in his heart and memory that he could feel and see the city without being in there. The poet's realistic descriptions of İstanbul's flora and fauna, and the inhabitants are also noteworthy. He refers to ordinary people, members of the working class, such as water carriers, fishermen, dockers and a 'dainty girl'. Ironically, the sweet spring breeze brings to the persona not the odour of flowers but the smell of sweat. Here, one cannot help but thinking of the resemblance between William Blake's 'London' and Orhan Veli's 'I am Listening to İstanbul' because both poets display a concern and sensitivity towards the hard lives of the working class. Despite the huge time gap between the composition of the two poems – Blake's poem was published nearly at the end of the eighteenth-century, and Orhan Veli's in the first decades of the twentieth century – both Blake's and Orhan Veli's awareness of the social problems of their eras resonates in their works; while Blake handled the social ills of his times in a dark, gloomy, pessimistic tone in 'London', Orhan Veli's depiction of the working-class people bears a rather humorous and playful note, resulting, perhaps, from the poet's belief in the revolutionary ideals and ideologies of the recently founded Turkish Republic. In the fourth stanza the speaker goes back to the ancient history of the city reflecting an awareness of past civilisations. Having been almost intoxicated with the idea of the glory of the bygone days, the speaker envisions an uninhabited mansion located on the shores of the Bosphorus. This stanza echoes a limited amount of nostalgia felt for the ancient civilisations cradled by İstanbul; however, the aspiration felt for the past is far greater in the works of Yahya Kemal and Tanpınar. In the last stanza, the city is personified as the speaker's beloved and is laden with female attributes.

The speaker knows every part of her body so well that although the lovers are physically apart from each other, the speaker feels her presence as if he were with her. Without touching her, he can feel her heart's palpitations, her brow, and her wet lips.

Regarding the comparison of Blake's and Orhan Veli's poems, one last discussion might be on the English translation of the word 'dainty girl' in the third stanza. In the original poem, Orhan Veli uses the noun 'yosma' while depicting her walking on the pavement accompanied by men's obscene words, songs, swears, and rude remarks; meanwhile, the rose she is holding in her hand drops into the ground. The fallen rose is often associated with her fallen condition because the word 'yosma', which actually means a young, beautiful, tempting woman, underwent a semantic change and came to be used for a "prostitute". In this respect, the affinity between the two poets' allusions to young prostitutes in their poems is interesting. Nevertheless, while Blake draws a very dark future awaiting the young desperate 'harlot' in 'London', Orhan Veli's 'yosma' whom Talat Halman elegantly translated as 'a dainty girl', just drops the rose in her hand and walks away, disregarding the abusive language of the men around.

Compared to the first two authors' treatment of İstanbul, Orhan Veli's approach to the cityscape appears to be much more passionate and realistic. For instance, in 'From Another Hill' Yahya Kemal described an idealised, almost idyllic İstanbul which was not so even during the poet's lifetime. Both Yahya Kemal's poem and Tanpınar's essay on İstanbul appear to be bearing an extreme amount of nostalgia for the past of the city. The two authors' melancholy image envisioned for İstanbul casts heavy shadows of doubt and uncertainty in the readers' minds about the future of İstanbul in the Republican Era.

Concluding Remarks

My readings and teaching experiences have shown me that the representation of cityscapes has been a concern of writers from all around the world throughout centuries. The everlasting interaction of the cityscape with the authors, the characters they create, and their intended audience encouraged me, like many others, to write articles, book chapters and finally this book focusing on the subject. Prior to my attempts at writing this book, including a comparative study of different authors' distinct attitudes towards the cities they exhibit in their works, I wrote, for instance, an article on the love-hate relationship related to the opposing sentiments that the cityscape evokes in James Joyce, and Orhan Pamuk.[47] The two urban landscapes in the said article are Dublin and İstanbul. While Joyce portrays Dublin life as a paralysing one condemning Dubliners to a shallow tasteless existence in his story collection, *Dubliners*, Orhan Pamuk in his novel, *İstanbul Memories and the City*, emphatically declares that he owes his aesthetic taste to İstanbul, to the city where he was born. The conclusion I drew was that it was Dublin and Istanbul, respectively, that shaped the two authors' literary formations; as Pamuk states in the opening pages of his novel, his love for İstanbul made him who he is; however, it was the hatred of the inartistic Dublin life that filled Joyce with the sense of weariness and provoked him to prefer a life in exile; yet, it should be noted that Dublin is the only setting in all of his

---

[47] Tekin, Kuğu. 'The Two Formative Forces in the Fiction of James Joyce and Orhan Pamuk'. Arcadia. Volume 50, Issue 2, pp. 410–419, ISSN (Online) 1613-0642, ISSN (Print) 003-7982, November 2015.

works. Likewise, it is observed that the oppressive political atmosphere prevailing in London might likely be the reason urging Blake to poeticise the suffering Londoners in his lyric 'London'. Wordsworth's description of the idealised beauty of London in the sonnet, 'Composed upon Westminster Bridge', might be considered a poetic escape from the environmental ills brought about by the Industrial Revolution. Rimbaud's prose poem, 'The Bridges', on the other hand, reflects a foreign poet's London impressions. Although Rimbaud's handling of the cityscape seems to be neutral, a cynical tone directed at British imperialism and national pride is discernible. While Calvino's surrealistic representation of Venice in his postmodern novel, *Invisible Cities*, is marked by the fictionalised Marco Polo's irresistible desire for a return to his glorious city, in Lord Byron's 'Canto IV Venice' the city is depicted as the site of a fading glory; the narrator reflects upon the city's monuments, piazzas and palaces as if they were the shadows, the remains of a victorious past that does not exist anymore. The Venice section of Henry James's *Italian Hours* exhibits a literary link of inspiration connecting the American author's picturesque portrayal of Venice to Yahya Kemal's and Ahmet Hamdi Tanpınar's descriptions of İstanbul in their works; it is observed that all the three authors took as their model the French Romantic poet Théophile Gautier and his vision of a painter in constructing the image of the urban landscape in their works. Another common point discerned in the works of Byron, James, Beyatlı and Tanpınar is the dominant melancholy tone the audience feels while reading the authors' impressions of the cityscapes. Regarding the description of the idealised beauty of the cityscape, Yahya Kemal's lyric, 'From Another Hill', is quite akin to Wordsworth's 'Composed upon Westminster Bridge'. Both poets' attitudes towards the nature of the cities they described are marked by adoration. Ahmet Hamdi Tanpınar's essay 'Istanbul', taken from his book titled *Five Cities*, rather appears to be a documentary recording the nature, architecture and arts, and the lifestyles and other idiosyncrasies of the various multi-cultural ethnicities populating İstanbul in the first half of the twentieth century and in the more distant past. In the work, İstanbul's melancholy image, which Tanpınar created together with his mentor and friend Yahya Kemal, holds a mirror to the inhabitants' sufferings and pains caused by World War I and the armistice years (1918–1923). The reason why the two Turkish authors' works embody a deep longing for a serene past is that both witnessed the turbulent years of the collapse of the Ottoman empire, the following armistice years, and ultimately the foundation years of the Republic of Turkey. Orhan Veli Kanık's 'I am Listening to İstanbul' ending Chapter 3 offers a realistic description of the city written in free verse. Orhan Veli's poem differs from the other poems hitherto discussed in terms of not just formal but also thematic qualities. The poetic persona of the poem appears to be in full possession of all the details related to İstanbul despite the physical distance between himself and the city, which is personified as a dearly loved woman. The speaker's memory and acute sense of hearing enable him to visualise the city without being present in İstanbul. As is seen, urban studies offer keen readers and scholars a rich source and a global platform that open new conversations on the ever-growing interaction between authors and the cities that, one way or another, haunt or infatuate them.

Bibliography

Abrams, M. H. *A Glossary of Literary Terms*. 6th ed., Harcourt Brace College Publishers, 1993.

Abrams, M. H., general editor. *The Norton Anthology of English Literature*. 6th ed., vol. 2, W. W. Norton, 1993.

Aydoğan, Fatih. 'Beş Şehir'in Hafıza Mekanları.' *Türklük Bilimi Araştırmaları*, no. 39, 2016, pp. 29–60, <https://dergipark.org.tr>.

Ackroyd, Peter. *Dan Leno and the Limehouse Golem*. Minerva, 1995.

Berry, David. 'Thematics of Hunger and Thirst in Rimbaud's Poetry.' *Romance Studies* 15 (2): 85–95. doi:10.1179/ros.1997.15.2.85.

Blake, William. 'London.' *The Norton Anthology of English Literature*, 6th ed., vol. 2, W. W. Norton, 1993, p. 39.

Bray, Patrick M. 'Orientations: Writing the Self in Nerval's *Voyage En Orient*.' *The Novel Map: Space and Subjectivity in Nineteenth-Century French Fiction*, Northwestern UP, 2013, pp. 65–84. *JSTOR*, <http://www.jstor.org/stable/j.ctt22727jt.11>.

Byron, George Gordon. 'Canto IV Venice.' *Childe Harold's Pilgrimage. The Norton Anthology of English Literature*, 6th ed., vol. 2, Norton, 1993, pp. 491–509.

Calvino, Italo. *Invisible Cities*. Cox & Wyman, 1997.

Calvino, Italo. 'On Invisible Cities.' *A Journal of Literature and Art*, no. 40, Oct. 2004, pp. 177–182, <https://www.jstor.org/stable/41808770>.

Carruthers, Mary J. *The Book of Memory*. Cambridge UP, 1992.

Doğan, Abide. 'Yahya Kemal'in İstanbul'u.' *Hacettepe Üniversitesi Türkiyat Araştırmaları (HÜTAD)*, no. 9, 2008, pp. 165–182.

Ebersolt, Jean. *Constantinople Byzantine Et Les Voyageurs du Levant*. Translated by İlhan Arda, Pera, 1996.

Eradam, Yusuf. 'My Sense of Belonging to İstanbul.' *IMAGES (IV): Images of the Other, Istanbul-Vienna-Venice*, International Conference Proceedings, Lit-Verlag, 2015, pp. 49–60.

Erol, Sibel. 'Orhan Veli: The Complete Poems.' Translated and edited by George Messo, *Translation and Literature*, vol. 28, no. 2–3, Edinburgh UP, 2019, pp. 398–408. <https://doi.org/10.3366/tal.2019.0402>.

Ferber, Michael. 'London and Its Politics.' *ELH*, vol. 48, no. 2, Johns Hopkins UP, 1981, pp. 310–338.

Frye, Northrop. *The Educated Imagination*. Indiana UP, 1964.

Gale, L. Robert. 'Henry James and Italy.' *Nineteenth-Century Fiction*, vol. 14, no. 2, University of California Press, 1959, pp. 157–170.

Gottdiener, Mark, Leslie Budd, and Panu Lehtovuori. *Key Concepts in Urban Studies*. Sage, 2016.

Güvenç, Özge. 'William Blake and William Wordsworth's Reactions to the Industrial Revolution.' *Çankaya University Journal of Humanities and Social Sciences*, vol. 11, no. 1, 2014, pp. 113–123.

Herrick, Robert. 'His Return to London.' *The Norton Anthology of English Literature*, 6th ed., vol. 1, Norton, 1993, p. 1366.

Hill, L. James. 'Experiments in the Narrative Consciousness: Byron, Wordsworth, and *Childe Harold*, Cantos 3 and 4.' *ELH*, vol. 53, no. 1, Johns Hopkins UP, 1986, pp. 121–140. *JSTOR*, jstor.org/stable/2873150.

James, Henry. *Italian Hours.* Grove Press Inc., 1909.

Kemal, Yahya. *Aziz İstanbul.* Yapı Kredi Yayınları, 2002.

Kerr, Greg. 'Rhetorics of Transformation in Rimbaud's *Illuminations*.' *Dix-Neuf: Journal of the Society of Dix-Neuviémistes*, vol. 14, no. 1, Routledge, 2010, pp. 20–32. <https://doi.org/10.1179/147873110X12669226709990>.

Kristeva, Julia. *Black Sun: Depression and Melancholia.* Translated by Leon S. Roudiez, Columbia UP, 1989.

Kumar, Sanjay. *Handbook of Economic Geography.* K. K. Publications, 2021.

Laven, David. 'Lord Byron, Count Daru, and Anglophone Myths of Venice in the Nineteenth Century.' *MDCCC 1800*, vol. 1, 2012, pp. 5–32, <https://edizionicafoscari.unive.it>.

Mack, Maynard, general editor. *The Norton Anthology of World Masterpieces.* 6th ed., vol. 2, W. W. Norton, 1992.

Manolescu-Oancea, Monica. "'We Have Botched Them and Patched Them': Modernity and Restoration in Henry James's *Italian Hours*." *e-Rea*, vol. 7, no. 2, 2010.

Mariani, Umberto. 'The Italian Experience of Henry James.' *Nineteenth-Century Fiction*, vol. 19, no. 3, University of California Press, 1964, pp. 237–254.

Miner, Paul. 'Blake's London: Times & Spaces.' *Studies in Romanticism*, vol. 41, no. 2, pp. 279–316, <https://www.jstor.org/stable/2560560>.

O'Keeffe, Bernard. "London' and 'Composed upon Westminster Bridge': Bernard O'Keeffe Compares and Contextualises Blake's and Wordsworth's Poems to Illuminate Aspects of Writing from the Romantic Era.' *The English Review*, vol. 17, no. 1, 2006, pp. 22–25.

Pamuk, Orhan. *İstanbul: Memories and the City.* Translated by Maureen Freely, Faber and Faber, 2006.

Pauly, Thomas H. "Henry James and the Travel Sketch: The Artistry of *Italian Hours*." *The Centennial Review*, vol. 19, no. 2, 1975, p. 108.

Pelletier-Israel, Aimée. 'Radical Realism: Rimbaud's Affinities with Impressionism.' *Mosaic: An Interdisciplinary Critical Journal*, vol. 25, no. 2, 1992, pp. 49–68. *JSTOR*, <https://www.jstor.org/stable/24780618>.

Preminger, Alex, and T. V. F. Brogan, editors. *The New Princeton Encyclopedia of Poetry and Poetics.* Princeton University Press, 1993.

Psarra, Sophia. 'Story-craft: The Imagination as Combinatorial Machine in Italo Calvino's *Invisible Cities*.' In *Venice Variations: Tracing the Architectural Imagination*, (pp. 139–173). UCL Press, 2018, <https://doi.org/10.2307/j.ctvqhspn.8>.

Rutherford, Andrew. 'The Influence of Hobhouse on *Childe Harold's Pilgrimage*, Canto IV.' *The Review of English Studies*, vol. 12, no. 48, Oxford UP, Nov. 1961, pp. 391–397. *JSTOR*, <https://www.jstor.org/stable/512107>.

Ryan, Robert. 'Politics, Discourse, Empire: Framed Knowledge in Italo Calvino's *Invisible Cities*.' *Interdisciplinary Literary Studies*, vol. 18, no. 2, pp. 222–237, <https://www.jstor.org/stable/10.5325/intelitestud.18.2.0222>.

Sandy, Mark. 'Thy Wreck a Glory: Venice, Subjectivity, and Temporality in Byron and Shelley and the Post-Romantic Imagination.' *Romanticism and Time: Literary Temporalities*, edited by Sophie Laniel-Musitelli and Celine Sabiron, Open Book Publishing House, 2021, pp. 205–224.

Sangster, Matthew. 'Coherence and Inclusion in the Life Writing of Romantic-period London.' *Life Writing*, vol. 14, no. 2, 2017, pp. 141–153. <https://doi.org/10.1080/14484528.2017.1291246>.

Sayers, Janet, and Nanette Monin. 'Blake's 'London': Diabolical Reading and Poetic Place in Organisational Theorising.' *Culture and Organization*, vol. 18, no. 1, 2012, pp. 1–13. <https://doi.org/10.1080/14759551.2011.631342>.

Schwenger, Peter. *The Tears of Things: Melancholy and Physical Objects.* University of Minnesota Press, 2016.

Shakespeare, William. *The Complete Works of William Shakespeare.* Edited by W. J. Craig, Pordes, 1952.

Shelley, Percy Bysshe. *The Lyrics and Minor Poems of Percy Bysshe Shelley - With a Prefatory Notice, By J. Skipsey.* Read Books, 2010.

Sivri, Medine, and Başak Özker. 'İstanbul as Poetic Space via the Works of Turkish and British Writers.' *Journal of Turkish Studies / Türklük Bilgisi Araştırmaları*, edited by Cemal Kafadar, Gönül A. Tekin, and Orçun Üçer, vol. 58, Department of Near Eastern Languages and Civilizations, Harvard University, 2022, pp. 259–277.

Stokes, Martin. 'Three Versions of Beloved İstanbul.' *The Republic of Love: Cultural Intimacy in Turkish Popular Music*, University of Chicago Press, 2010, pp. 147–189.

Stokes, C. R. 'Sign, Sensation and the Body in Wordsworth's Residence in London.' *European Romantic Review*, vol. 23, no. 2, 2012, pp. 203–223. <https://doi.org/10.1080/10509585.2012.653281>.

Strachey, James, editor. 'On Transience.' *The Standard Edition of the Complete Psychological Works of Sigmund Freud: On the History of the Psycho-Analytic Movement, Papers on Metapsychology and Other Works*, vol. 14, 1914–1916, The Hogarth Press and the Institute of Psychology, 1957, pp. 303–309.

———. 'Mourning and Melancholia.' *The Standard Edition of the Complete Psychological Works of Sigmund Freud: On the History of the Psycho-Analytic Movement, Papers on Metapsychology and Other Works*, vol. 14, 1914–1916, The Hogarth Press and the Institute of Psychology, 1957, pp. 237–239.

Sudjic, Deyan. *The Language of Cities.* Penguin Random House, 2016.

Tanpınar, Ahmet Hamdi. *Tanpınar's Five Cities.* Translated by Ruth Christie, Anthem Press, 2018.

Tekin, Kuğu. 'Dublin and Istanbul: The Two Formative Forces in the Fiction of James Joyce and Orhan Pamuk.' *Arcadia*, vol. 50, no. 2, 2015, pp. 410–419.

———. 'Orhan Pamuk's İstanbul Carved in His Memory as a Source of Melancholy.' *Folklore Literature*, Cyprus International University, 2018, pp. 203–212. <https://doi.org/10.22559/folklore.194>.

————. 'Mapping London in Peter Ackroyd's *Dan Leno and the Limehouse Golem*: Promenades into a Murderer's Mind.' *Ankara University: Journal of the Faculty of Languages and History-Geography*, vol. 58, no. 2, 2018, pp. 1522–1534. <https://doi.org/10.33171/dtcfjournal.2018.58.2.17>.

————. 'Marginalised Flaneurs in Venice in the Works of Mann, Winterson, and Ishiguro.' *Synergy I: Marginalisation, Discrimination, Isolation and Existence in Literature*, edited by A. Nejat Töngür and Yıldıray Çevik, Peter Lang, 2021, pp. 95–116.

Weitzman, J. Arthur. 'Eighteenth-Century London: Urban Paradise or Fallen City.' *Journal of the History of Ideas*, vol. 36, no. 3, July-Sept. 1975, pp. 469–480. University of Pennsylvania Press, <https://www.jstor.org/stable/2708657>.

Wordsworth, William. 'Composed upon Westminster Bridge.' *The Norton Anthology of English Literature*, 6th ed., vol. 1, Norton & Company, 1993, p. 198.

Appendices

Appendix A

William Blake: 'Jerusalem'

And did those feet in ancient time
Walk upon England's mountains green:
And was the holy Lamb of God,
On England's pleasant pastures seen!

And did the Countenance Divine,
Shine forth upon our clouded hills?
And was Jerusalem builded here,
Among these dark Satanic Mills?
Bring me my Bow of burning gold:
Bring me my arrows of desire:
Bring me my Spear: O clouds unfold!
Bring me my Chariot of fire!

I will not cease from Mental Fight,
Nor shall my sword sleep in my hand:
Till we have built Jerusalem,
In England's green & pleasant Land.

Appendix B

Lord Byron: 'Ode on Venice'

I.
Oh Venice! Venice! when thy marble walls
Are level with the waters, there shall be
A cry of nations o'er thy sunken halls,

A loud lament along the sweeping sea!
If I, a northern wanderer, weep for thee,
What should thy sons do? – anything but weep
And yet they only murmur in their sleep.
In contrast with their fathers – as the slime,
The dull green ooze of the receding deep,
Is with the dashing of the spring-tide foam
That drives the sailor shipless to his home,
Are they to those that were; and thus they creep,
Crouching and crab-like, through their sapping streets.
Oh! Agony-that centuries should reap
No mellower harvest! Thirteen hundred years
Of wealth and glory turn'd to dust and tears;
And every monument the stranger meets,
Church, palace, pillar, as a mourner greets;
And even the Lion all subdued appears,
And the harsh sound of the barbarian
With dull and daily dissonance, repeats
The echo of thy tyrant's voice along
The soft waves, once all musical to song,
That heaved beneath the moonlight with the throng
Of gondolas – and to the busy hum
Of cheerful creatures, whose most sinful deeds
Were but the overbeating of the heart,
And flow of too much happiness, which needs
The aid of age to turn its course apart
From the luxuriant and voluptuous flood
Of sweet sensations, battling with the blood.
But these are better than the gloomy errors,
The weeds of nations in their last decay,
When Vice walks forth with her unsoften'd terrors,
And Mirth is madness, and but smiles to slay;
And Hope is nothing but a false delay,
The sick man's lightning half an hour ere death,
When Faintness, the last mortal birth of Pain,
And apathy of limb, the dull beginning
Of the cold staggering race which Death is winning,
Steals vein by vein and pulse by pulse away;
Yet so relieving the o'er-tortured clay,
To him appears renewal of his breath,
And freedom the mere numbness of his chain;
And then he talks of life, and how again
He feels his spirit soaring – albeit weak,
And of the fresher air, which he would seek:

And as he whispers knows not that he gasps,
That his thin finger feels not what it claps,
And so the film comes o'er him, and the dizzy
Chamber swims round and round, and shadows busy,
At which he vainly catches, flit and gleam,
Till the last rattle chokes the strangled scream,
And all is ice and blackness, – and the earth
That which it was the moment ere our birth.

II.
There is no hope for nations! – Search the page
Of many thousand years – the daily scene,
The flow and ebb of each recurring age,
The everlasting to be which hath been
Hath taught us nought, or little: still we lean
On things that rot beneath our weight, and wear
Our strength away in wrestling with the air:
For 'tis our nature strikes us down: the beasts
Slaughter 'd in hourly hecatombs for feasts
Are of as high an order – they must go
Even where their driver goads them though to slaughter.
Ye men, who pour your blood for kings as water,
What have they given your children in return?
A heritage of servitude and woes,
A blindfold bondage, where your hire is blows.
What! do not yet the red-hot ploughshares burn,
O'er which you stumble in a false ordeal,
And deem this proof of loyalty the real;
Kissing the hand that guides you to your scars,
And glorying as you tread the glowing bars?
All that your sires have left you, all that Time
Bequeaths of free, and History of sublime,
Spring from a different theme! Ye see and read,
Admire and sigh, and then succumb and bleed!
Save the few spirits who, despite of all,
And worse than all, the sudden crimes engender'd
By the down-thundering of the prison wall,
And thirst to swallow the sweet waters tender'd,
Gushing from Freedom's fountains, when the crowd,
Madden'd with centuries of drought, are loud,
And trample on each other to obtain
The cup which brings oblivion of a chain
Heavy and sore, in which long yoked they plough'd
The sand, – or if there sprung the yellow grain,

'Twos not for them, their necks were too much bow'd,
And their dead palates chew'd the cud of pain:
Yes! the few spirits, who, despite of deeds
Which they abhor, confound not with the cause
Those momentary starts from Nature's laws,
Which, like the pestilence and earthquake, smite
But for a term, then pass, and leave the earth
With all her seasons to repair the blight
With a few summers, and again put forth
Cities and generations – fair, when free
For, Tyranny, there blooms no bud for thee!

III.
Glory and Empire! once upon these towers
With Freedom – godlike Triad! how ye sate!
The league of mightiest nations, in those hours
When Venice was an envy, might abate,
But did not quench her spirit, in her fate
All were enwrapp'd: the feasted monarchs knew
And loved their hostess, nor could learn to hate,
Although they humbled – with the kingly few
The many felt, for from all days and climes
She was the voyager's worship; even her crimes
Were of the softer order – born of Love,
She drank no blood, nor fatten'd on the dead,
But gladden'd where her harmless conquests spread;
For these restored the Cross, that from above
Hallow'd her sheltering banners, which incessant
Flew between earth and the unholy Crescent,
Which, if it waned and dwindled, Earth may thank
The city it has clothed in chains, which clank
Now, creaking in the ears of those who owe
The name of Freedom to her glorious struggles;
Yet she but shares with them a common woe,
And call'd the 'kingdom' of a conquering foe,
But knows what all – and, most of all, we know –
With what set gilded terms a tyrant juggles!
The name of Commonwealth is past and gone
O'er the three fractions of the groaning globe;
Venice is crush'd, and Holland deigns to own
A sceptre, and endures the purple robe;
If the free Switzer yet bestrides alone
His chainless mountains, 'tis but for a time,
For tyranny of late is cunning grown,

And in its own good season tramples down
The sparkles of our ashes. One great clime,
Whose vigorous offspring by dividing ocean
Are kept apart and nursed in the devotion
Of Freedom, which their fathers fought for, and
Bequeath'd – a heritage of heart and hand,
And proud distinction from each other land,
Whose sons must bow them at a monarch's motion,
As if his senseless sceptre were a wand
Full of the magic of exploded science –
Still one great clime, in full and free defiance,
Yet rears her crest, unconquer'd and sublime,
Above the far Atlantic! – She has taught
Her Esau – brethren that the haughty flag,
The floating fence of Albion's feebler crag,
May strike to those whose red right hands have bought
Rights cheaply earn'd with blood. Stilt, still, for ever,
Better, though each man's life – blood were a river,
That it should flow, and overflow, than creep
Through thousand lazy channels in our veins
 Damm'd like the dull canal with locks and chains,
And moving, as a sick man in his sleep,
Three paces, and then faltering: better be
Where the extinguish'd Spartans still are free,
In their proud charnel of Thermopylae,
Than stagnate in our marsh, – or o'er the deep
Fly, and one current to the ocean add,
One spirit to the souls our fathers had,
One freeman more, America, to thee!

Appendix C
Yahya Kemal Beyatlı: 'From Another Hill'

Sana dün bir tepeden baktım aziz İstanbul!
Görmedim gezmediğim, sevmediğim hiçbir yer.
Ömrüm oldukça, gönül tahtıma keyfince kurul!
Sade bir semtini sevmek bile bir ömre değer.

Nice revnaklı şehirler görülür dünyada,
Lakin efsunlu güzellikleri sensin yaratan.
Yaşamıştır derim, en hoş ve uzun rü'yada
Sende çok yıl yaşayan, sende ölen, sende yatan.

Appendix D

Orhan Veli Kanık: 'İstanbul'u Dinliyorum'

İstanbul'u dinliyorum, gözlerim kapalı
Önce hafiften bir rüzgâr esiyor;
Yavaş yavaş sallanıyor
Yapraklar, ağaçlarda;
Uzaklarda, çok uzaklarda,
Sucuların hiç durmayan çıngırakları
İstanbul'u dinliyorum, gözlerim kapalı.

İstanbul'u dinliyorum, gözlerim kapalı;
Kuşlar geçiyor, derken;
Yükseklerden, sürü sürü, çığlık çığlık.
Ağlar çekiliyor dalyanlarda;
Bir kadının suya değiyor ayakları
İstanbul'u dinliyorum, gözlerim kapalı.

İstanbul'u dinliyorum, gözlerim kapalı;
Serin serin Kapalıçarşı
Cıvıl cıvıl Mahmutpaşa
Güvercin dolu avlular
Çekiç sesleri geliyor doklardan
Güzelim bahar rüzgârında ter kokuları;
İstanbul'u dinliyorum, gözlerim kapalı.
İstanbul'u dinliyorum, gözlerim kapalı;
Başımda eski âlemlerin sarhoşluğu
Loş kayıkhaneleriyle bir yalı;
Dinmiş lodosların uğultusu içinde
İstanbul'u dinliyorum, gözlerim kapalı.

İstanbul'u dinliyorum, gözlerim kapalı;
Bir yosma geçiyor kaldırımdan;
Küfürler, şarkılar, türküler, laf atmalar.
Bir şey düşüyor elinden yere;
Bir gül olmalı;
İstanbul'u dinliyorum, gözlerim kapalı.

İstanbul'u dinliyorum, gözlerim kapalı;
Bir kuş çırpınıyor eteklerinde;
Alnın sıcak mı, değil mi, biliyorum;
Dudakların ıslak mı, değil mi, biliyorum;

Beyaz bir ay doğuyor fıstıkların arkasından
Kalbinin vuruşundan anlıyorum;
İstanbul'u dinliyorum.

Appendix E
Antoine Ignace Melling

Melling (1763–1831) was a French painter and architect. He studied architecture and mathematics. In 1784, Melling moved to İstanbul as attaché to the Russian Embassy and lived in that city for eighteen years. He was architect to Sultan Seim III and his sister Hatice, with whom he maintained a close relationship. Melling designed the gardens and the interior of Hatice Sultan's Palace in Ortaköy, and the interior of the newly built palace in Defterdar Burnu, in neoclassical style, as well as jewellery and clothes. Melling's best known İstanbul engravings are collected in the work titled *Voyage Pittoresque de Constantinople et des rives du Bosphore*. In the work, İstanbul, which was then the Ottoman capital, its natural landscape as well as monuments and everyday life unfolded before the eyes of the Europeans in an unparalleled way. Melling saw İstanbul as an Ottoman citizen but was able to paint it as an insightful Western European. (Ioli Vingopoulou <https://eng.travelogues.gr>)

Appendix F
Thomas Allom

Allom began his career working as an architect (between 1819 and 1826), and after seven years he went on to study at the Royal Academy Schools where he worked on designs for churches, workhouses and a military asylum. While at the Royal Academy, Allom began to exhibit his work, a practice he continued until the end of his life in 1834. Allom was one of the founders of the Royal Institute of British Architects, where he worked on various projects, including the Houses of Parliament, Highclere and the Thames Embankment. The majority of Allom's works are well suited to reproduction and were made with the engraver in mind. He travelled extensively and over the course of his career contributed hundreds of illustrations for travel and topographical books. <https://www.nga.gov>